50 Baking Made Simple Recipes for Home

By: Kelly Johnson

Table of Contents

- Chocolate Chip Cookies
- Banana Bread
- Vanilla Cupcakes
- Lemon Bars
- Blueberry Muffins
- Carrot Cake
- Brownies
- Apple Pie
- Pumpkin Bread
- Red Velvet Cake
- Shortbread Cookies
- Cinnamon Rolls
- Cheesecake
- Scones
- Chocolate Cake
- Peanut Butter Cookies
- Strawberry Shortcake
- Oatmeal Raisin Cookies
- Pound Cake
- Gingerbread Cookies
- Key Lime Pie
- Biscotti
- Pecan Pie
- Coconut Macaroons
- Raspberry Tart
- Coffee Cake
- Linzer Cookies
- Eclairs
- Angel Food Cake
- Focaccia Bread
- Cheese Danish
- Macarons
- Rugelach
- Baklava
- Lemon Poppy Seed Muffins
- Almond Biscotti

- Fruitcake
- Chocolate Souffle
- Cherry Pie
- Irish Soda Bread
- Mille-Feuille (Napoleon)
- Palmiers
- Lemon Pound Cake
- Popovers
- Cannoli
- Black Forest Cake
- Buttermilk Biscuits
- Danish Pastry
- Sticky Buns
- Pita Bread

Chocolate Chip Cookies

Ingredients:

- 1 cup (2 sticks) unsalted butter, softened
- 3/4 cup granulated sugar
- 3/4 cup packed brown sugar
- 1 teaspoon vanilla extract
- 2 large eggs
- 2 1/4 cups all-purpose flour
- 1 teaspoon baking soda
- 1/2 teaspoon salt
- 2 cups semisweet chocolate chips

Instructions:

1. Preheat your oven to 375°F (190°C). Line a baking sheet with parchment paper or lightly grease it.
2. In a large mixing bowl, cream together the softened butter, granulated sugar, brown sugar, and vanilla extract until smooth and creamy.
3. Beat in the eggs, one at a time, until well incorporated.
4. In a separate bowl, whisk together the flour, baking soda, and salt.
5. Gradually add the flour mixture to the wet ingredients, mixing until just combined.
6. Stir in the chocolate chips until evenly distributed throughout the dough.
7. Drop rounded tablespoons of dough onto the prepared baking sheet, spacing them about 2 inches apart.
8. Bake in the preheated oven for 9 to 11 minutes, or until the edges are golden brown. The centers may still look slightly soft.
9. Remove from the oven and let the cookies cool on the baking sheet for 2 minutes, then transfer them to a wire rack to cool completely.
10. Enjoy your delicious homemade chocolate chip cookies!

Makes about 3 dozen cookies, depending on size.

Banana Bread

Ingredients:

- 3 ripe bananas, mashed (about 1 1/2 cups)
- 1/3 cup unsalted butter, melted
- 3/4 cup granulated sugar
- 1 egg, beaten
- 1 teaspoon vanilla extract
- 1 teaspoon baking soda
- Pinch of salt
- 1 1/2 cups all-purpose flour

Optional Add-Ins:

- 1/2 cup chopped nuts (walnuts or pecans)
- 1/2 cup chocolate chips

Instructions:

1. Preheat your oven to 350°F (175°C). Grease a 9x5 inch loaf pan or line it with parchment paper.
2. In a mixing bowl, mash the ripe bananas with a fork or potato masher until smooth.
3. Stir the melted butter into the mashed bananas.
4. Mix in the sugar, beaten egg, and vanilla extract until well combined.
5. Add the baking soda and salt to the mixture and stir.
6. Gradually add the flour to the wet ingredients, mixing gently until just combined. Do not overmix. If you're adding nuts or chocolate chips, fold them in at this stage.
7. Pour the batter into the prepared loaf pan, spreading it out evenly.
8. Bake in the preheated oven for 60 to 65 minutes, or until a toothpick inserted into the center comes out clean.
9. Allow the banana bread to cool in the pan for about 10 minutes, then remove it from the pan and transfer it to a wire rack to cool completely.
10. Slice and enjoy your delicious homemade banana bread!

This recipe yields one loaf of banana bread, which is moist, flavorful, and perfect for breakfast or a snack.

Vanilla Cupcakes

Ingredients:

- 1 1/4 cups all-purpose flour
- 1 1/4 teaspoons baking powder
- 1/2 teaspoon baking soda
- 1/2 teaspoon salt
- 2 large eggs, at room temperature
- 3/4 cup granulated sugar
- 1/2 cup unsalted butter, melted and cooled slightly
- 1 1/2 teaspoons vanilla extract
- 1/2 cup sour cream
- 1/2 cup milk

Instructions:

1. Preheat your oven to 350°F (175°C). Line a muffin tin with cupcake liners.
2. In a medium bowl, whisk together the flour, baking powder, baking soda, and salt. Set aside.
3. In a large bowl, whisk the eggs and granulated sugar together until well combined and slightly thickened.
4. Add the melted butter and vanilla extract to the egg mixture, whisking until smooth.
5. Stir in the sour cream until well combined.
6. Gradually add half of the flour mixture to the wet ingredients, stirring gently until just combined.
7. Add the milk, stirring until smooth.
8. Add the remaining flour mixture and stir until the batter is smooth and well combined. Be careful not to overmix.
9. Divide the batter evenly among the cupcake liners, filling each about 2/3 full.
10. Bake in the preheated oven for 18-20 minutes, or until a toothpick inserted into the center comes out clean.
11. Remove from the oven and allow the cupcakes to cool in the pan for a few minutes before transferring them to a wire rack to cool completely.

Optional Frosting:

For a classic vanilla buttercream frosting, beat 1/2 cup (1 stick) of unsalted butter (at room temperature) until creamy. Gradually add 2 cups of powdered sugar, beating until smooth and fluffy. Add 1-2 tablespoons of milk and 1 teaspoon of vanilla extract, and beat until light and creamy. Frost the cooled cupcakes as desired.

Enjoy your homemade vanilla cupcakes!

Lemon Bars

Ingredients:

For the Crust:

- 1 cup all-purpose flour
- 1/4 cup powdered sugar
- 1/2 cup unsalted butter, cold and cut into small pieces

For the Lemon Filling:

- 4 large eggs
- 1 1/2 cups granulated sugar
- 1/3 cup fresh lemon juice (about 2-3 lemons)
- 1 tablespoon lemon zest (from about 2 lemons)
- 1/4 cup all-purpose flour
- 1/2 teaspoon baking powder
- Powdered sugar, for dusting (optional)

Instructions:

1. Preheat your oven to 350°F (175°C). Grease or line with parchment paper a 9x13-inch baking pan.
2. **Prepare the Crust:**
    - In a medium bowl, whisk together the flour and powdered sugar.
    - Cut in the cold butter using a pastry cutter or fork until the mixture resembles coarse crumbs and starts to hold together.
    - Press the mixture evenly into the bottom of the prepared baking pan.
    - Bake the crust in the preheated oven for 15-20 minutes, or until lightly golden brown.
3. **Prepare the Lemon Filling:**
    - In a large bowl, whisk together the eggs and granulated sugar until well combined.
    - Add the lemon juice and lemon zest, and whisk until smooth.
    - In a separate bowl, whisk together the flour and baking powder.
    - Gradually add the flour mixture to the lemon mixture, whisking until smooth and well combined.
4. **Assemble and Bake:**
    - Pour the lemon filling over the baked crust, spreading it evenly with a spatula.
    - Return the pan to the oven and bake for an additional 20-25 minutes, or until the filling is set and lightly golden brown on top.
5. **Cool and Serve:**
    - Allow the lemon bars to cool completely in the pan on a wire rack.
    - Once cooled, dust with powdered sugar if desired.

- Cut into squares and serve.

These lemon bars are best stored in an airtight container in the refrigerator. Enjoy the tangy sweetness of these homemade treats!

Blueberry Muffins

Ingredients:

- 1/2 cup (1 stick) unsalted butter, melted and cooled slightly
- 1 cup granulated sugar
- 2 large eggs
- 1 teaspoon vanilla extract
- 1/2 cup milk (whole milk or buttermilk preferred)
- 2 cups all-purpose flour
- 2 teaspoons baking powder
- 1/2 teaspoon baking soda
- 1/2 teaspoon salt
- 1 1/2 cups fresh or frozen blueberries (if using frozen, do not thaw)

Instructions:

1. Preheat your oven to 375°F (190°C). Line a muffin tin with paper liners or grease the muffin cups.
2. In a large bowl, whisk together the melted butter and granulated sugar until well combined.
3. Add the eggs one at a time, whisking well after each addition.
4. Whisk in the vanilla extract and milk until smooth.
5. In a separate bowl, whisk together the flour, baking powder, baking soda, and salt.
6. Gradually add the dry ingredients to the wet ingredients, mixing gently until just combined. Do not overmix; the batter should be lumpy.
7. Gently fold in the blueberries until evenly distributed throughout the batter.
8. Divide the batter evenly among the muffin cups, filling each about 3/4 full.
9. Optional: Sprinkle a little granulated sugar on top of each muffin before baking for a slightly crunchy top.
10. Bake in the preheated oven for 18-20 minutes, or until the muffins are golden brown and a toothpick inserted into the center comes out clean.
11. Remove from the oven and let the muffins cool in the pan for 5 minutes before transferring them to a wire rack to cool completely.
12. Enjoy your homemade blueberry muffins warm or at room temperature!

These muffins are best enjoyed fresh but can be stored in an airtight container at room temperature for up to 3 days or frozen for longer storage.

Carrot Cake

Ingredients:

For the Cake:

- 2 cups all-purpose flour
- 2 teaspoons baking powder
- 1 1/2 teaspoons baking soda
- 1/2 teaspoon salt
- 1 teaspoon ground cinnamon
- 1/2 teaspoon ground nutmeg
- 1/2 teaspoon ground ginger
- 1 cup granulated sugar
- 1 cup brown sugar, packed
- 1 cup vegetable oil or melted coconut oil
- 4 large eggs
- 2 teaspoons vanilla extract
- 3 cups grated carrots (about 4-5 medium carrots)
- 1 cup chopped nuts (walnuts or pecans), optional
- 1/2 cup crushed pineapple, drained (optional)

For the Cream Cheese Frosting:

- 8 oz (1 package) cream cheese, softened
- 1/2 cup unsalted butter, softened
- 4 cups powdered sugar
- 1 teaspoon vanilla extract

Instructions:

1. Preheat your oven to 350°F (175°C). Grease and flour two 9-inch round cake pans or line them with parchment paper.
2. **Prepare the Cake:**
    - In a large bowl, whisk together the flour, baking powder, baking soda, salt, cinnamon, nutmeg, and ginger until well combined.
    - In another bowl, whisk together the granulated sugar, brown sugar, oil, eggs, and vanilla extract until smooth.
    - Gradually add the wet ingredients to the dry ingredients, stirring until just combined.
    - Fold in the grated carrots, chopped nuts (if using), and crushed pineapple (if using) until evenly distributed in the batter.
3. Divide the batter evenly between the prepared cake pans.
4. Bake in the preheated oven for 25-30 minutes, or until a toothpick inserted into the center comes out clean.

5. Remove the cakes from the oven and let them cool in the pans for 10 minutes before transferring them to a wire rack to cool completely.
6. **Prepare the Cream Cheese Frosting:**
    - In a large bowl, beat the softened cream cheese and butter together until smooth and creamy.
    - Gradually add the powdered sugar, one cup at a time, beating well after each addition.
    - Add the vanilla extract and beat until the frosting is smooth and fluffy.
7. **Assemble the Cake:**
    - Place one cake layer on a serving plate or cake stand.
    - Spread a layer of cream cheese frosting evenly over the top.
    - Place the second cake layer on top and spread the remaining frosting over the top and sides of the cake.
8. Optional: Decorate the top of the cake with additional chopped nuts or a sprinkle of cinnamon.
9. Chill the cake in the refrigerator for at least 30 minutes before slicing and serving.
10. Enjoy your homemade carrot cake with a deliciously creamy cream cheese frosting!

Carrot cake can be stored covered in the refrigerator for up to 5 days. Allow it to come to room temperature before serving for the best taste and texture.

Brownies

Ingredients:

- 1 cup (2 sticks) unsalted butter
- 2 cups granulated sugar
- 4 large eggs
- 1 teaspoon vanilla extract
- 1 cup all-purpose flour
- 3/4 cup unsweetened cocoa powder
- 1/2 teaspoon salt
- 1/2 teaspoon baking powder

Optional Add-Ins:

- 1 cup chocolate chips
- 1 cup chopped nuts (walnuts or pecans)

Instructions:

1. Preheat your oven to 350°F (175°C). Grease a 9x13-inch baking pan or line it with parchment paper.
2. In a medium saucepan, melt the butter over medium heat. Stir in the granulated sugar until well combined. Remove from heat and let the mixture cool slightly.
3. In a large bowl, whisk together the eggs and vanilla extract.
4. Gradually add the slightly cooled butter-sugar mixture to the eggs, whisking constantly until smooth.
5. In a separate bowl, sift together the flour, cocoa powder, salt, and baking powder.
6. Gradually add the dry ingredients to the wet ingredients, stirring gently until just combined. Do not overmix.
7. If using, fold in the chocolate chips and/or chopped nuts until evenly distributed in the batter.
8. Pour the batter into the prepared baking pan, spreading it out evenly with a spatula.
9. Bake in the preheated oven for 25-30 minutes, or until a toothpick inserted into the center comes out with a few moist crumbs.
10. Remove from the oven and let the brownies cool completely in the pan on a wire rack before slicing into squares.
11. Enjoy your homemade brownies! They're perfect served warm with a scoop of ice cream or simply on their own.

These brownies can be stored in an airtight container at room temperature for up to 3 days, or in the refrigerator for longer storage.

Apple Pie

Ingredients:

For the Pie Crust:

- 2 1/2 cups all-purpose flour
- 1 teaspoon salt
- 1 tablespoon granulated sugar
- 1 cup unsalted butter, cold and cut into small cubes
- 1/4 to 1/2 cup ice water

For the Apple Filling:

- 6 cups thinly sliced peeled apples (use a mix of sweet and tart varieties like Granny Smith and Honeycrisp)
- 3/4 cup granulated sugar
- 2 tablespoons all-purpose flour
- 1 teaspoon ground cinnamon
- 1/4 teaspoon ground nutmeg
- 1/4 teaspoon salt
- 1 tablespoon lemon juice
- 1 tablespoon unsalted butter, cut into small pieces

Egg Wash:

- 1 egg
- 1 tablespoon milk or water

Instructions:

1. **Prepare the Pie Crust:**
   - In a large bowl, whisk together the flour, salt, and sugar.
   - Add the cold butter cubes to the flour mixture. Use a pastry cutter or your fingers to cut the butter into the flour until the mixture resembles coarse crumbs with some larger pea-sized pieces of butter.
   - Gradually add the ice water, 1 tablespoon at a time, mixing gently with a fork or your hands until the dough just begins to come together. Be careful not to overwork the dough.
   - Divide the dough into two equal portions and shape each portion into a flat disc. Wrap each disc tightly in plastic wrap and refrigerate for at least 1 hour, or overnight.
2. **Prepare the Apple Filling:**
   - In a large bowl, toss the sliced apples with the granulated sugar, flour, cinnamon, nutmeg, salt, and lemon juice until well combined. Set aside.
3. **Assemble and Bake the Pie:**

- Preheat your oven to 400°F (200°C). Place a baking sheet in the oven to preheat as well (this helps to cook the bottom crust evenly).
- On a lightly floured surface, roll out one disc of chilled dough into a circle about 12 inches in diameter. Carefully transfer the rolled dough to a 9-inch pie dish, gently pressing it into the bottom and sides.
- Spoon the apple filling into the prepared pie crust, mounding it slightly in the center. Dot the top of the filling with small pieces of butter.
- Roll out the second disc of dough into a circle about 12 inches in diameter. Place it over the filling. Trim any excess dough hanging over the edges, leaving about a 1-inch overhang. Pinch the edges of the top and bottom crusts together and fold the overhang under itself, creating a thick edge that rests on the lip of the pie dish.
- Flute the edges of the pie crust or crimp with a fork to seal. Cut a few small slits in the top crust to allow steam to escape during baking.

4. **Egg Wash:**
   - In a small bowl, whisk together the egg and milk (or water). Brush the top crust with the egg wash.
5. **Bake the Pie:**
   - Place the pie on the preheated baking sheet in the oven. Bake for 20 minutes at 400°F (200°C), then reduce the oven temperature to 350°F (175°C). Continue baking for an additional 35-45 minutes, or until the crust is golden brown and the filling is bubbly.
6. **Cool and Serve:**
   - Allow the pie to cool on a wire rack for at least 2 hours before serving to allow the filling to set.
7. **Enjoy your homemade apple pie!** Serve warm or at room temperature, optionally with a scoop of vanilla ice cream or a dollop of whipped cream.

Store any leftovers covered at room temperature for up to 2 days, or in the refrigerator for longer storage.

Pumpkin Bread

Ingredients:

- 1 3/4 cups all-purpose flour
- 1 teaspoon baking soda
- 1/2 teaspoon baking powder
- 1 teaspoon ground cinnamon
- 1/2 teaspoon ground nutmeg
- 1/2 teaspoon ground cloves
- 1/2 teaspoon salt
- 1/2 cup unsalted butter, softened
- 1 1/2 cups granulated sugar
- 2 large eggs
- 1 cup canned pumpkin puree (not pumpkin pie filling)
- 1/3 cup water
- 1 teaspoon vanilla extract

Optional Add-Ins:

- 1/2 cup chopped nuts (walnuts or pecans)
- 1/2 cup raisins or dried cranberries
- 1/2 cup chocolate chips

Instructions:

1. Preheat your oven to 350°F (175°C). Grease and flour a 9x5-inch loaf pan or line it with parchment paper.
2. In a medium bowl, whisk together the flour, baking soda, baking powder, cinnamon, nutmeg, cloves, and salt until well combined. Set aside.
3. In a large bowl, cream together the softened butter and granulated sugar until light and fluffy.
4. Add the eggs one at a time, beating well after each addition.
5. Stir in the pumpkin puree, water, and vanilla extract until smooth and well combined.
6. Gradually add the dry ingredients to the wet ingredients, mixing until just combined. Do not overmix.
7. If using, fold in the optional add-ins such as chopped nuts, raisins, or chocolate chips until evenly distributed in the batter.
8. Pour the batter into the prepared loaf pan, spreading it out evenly with a spatula.
9. Bake in the preheated oven for 60-70 minutes, or until a toothpick inserted into the center comes out clean.
10. Remove from the oven and let the pumpkin bread cool in the pan for 10 minutes before transferring it to a wire rack to cool completely.
11. Slice and enjoy your homemade pumpkin bread!

This pumpkin bread can be stored in an airtight container at room temperature for up to 3 days, or in the refrigerator for longer freshness. It also freezes well for longer-term storage.

Red Velvet Cake

Ingredients:

For the Cake:

- 2 1/2 cups all-purpose flour
- 1 1/2 cups granulated sugar
- 1 teaspoon baking soda
- 1 teaspoon cocoa powder
- 1 teaspoon salt
- 2 large eggs
- 1 1/2 cups vegetable oil
- 1 cup buttermilk, at room temperature
- 1 tablespoon red food coloring (gel or liquid)
- 1 teaspoon vanilla extract
- 1 teaspoon white vinegar

For the Cream Cheese Frosting:

- 16 oz (2 packages) cream cheese, softened
- 1/2 cup unsalted butter, softened
- 4 cups powdered sugar
- 1 teaspoon vanilla extract

Instructions:

1. **Preheat your oven to 350°F (175°C).** Grease and flour two 9-inch round cake pans or line them with parchment paper.
2. **Prepare the Cake:**
   - In a large bowl, sift together the flour, sugar, baking soda, cocoa powder, and salt.
   - In another bowl, whisk together the eggs, vegetable oil, buttermilk, red food coloring, vanilla extract, and white vinegar until smooth and well combined.
   - Gradually add the wet ingredients to the dry ingredients, mixing until smooth and combined. Be careful not to overmix.
3. **Bake the Cake:**
   - Divide the batter evenly between the prepared cake pans.
   - Bake in the preheated oven for 25-30 minutes, or until a toothpick inserted into the center of the cakes comes out clean.
   - Remove from the oven and let the cakes cool in the pans for 10 minutes before transferring them to a wire rack to cool completely.
4. **Prepare the Cream Cheese Frosting:**
   - In a large bowl, beat the softened cream cheese and butter together until smooth and creamy.

- Gradually add the powdered sugar, one cup at a time, beating well after each addition.
- Add the vanilla extract and beat until the frosting is smooth and fluffy.
5. **Assemble the Cake:**
    - Place one cake layer on a serving plate or cake stand.
    - Spread a layer of cream cheese frosting evenly over the top.
    - Place the second cake layer on top and frost the top and sides of the cake with the remaining frosting.
    - Optional: Use a spatula or piping bag to create decorative swirls or patterns on the cake.
6. **Chill and Serve:**
    - Chill the cake in the refrigerator for at least 30 minutes before slicing and serving to allow the frosting to set.
7. **Enjoy your homemade red velvet cake!** Serve slices at room temperature for the best taste and texture.

Store any leftover cake covered in the refrigerator for up to 3 days. Bring to room temperature before serving.

Shortbread Cookies

Ingredients:

- 1 cup (2 sticks) unsalted butter, softened
- 1/2 cup granulated sugar
- 2 cups all-purpose flour
- 1/4 teaspoon salt (if using unsalted butter)
- Optional: 1 teaspoon vanilla extract or other flavorings (such as almond extract or lemon zest)

Instructions:

1. Preheat your oven to 350°F (175°C). Line a baking sheet with parchment paper or lightly grease it.
2. In a large bowl, cream together the softened butter and granulated sugar until smooth and creamy.
3. If using, stir in the vanilla extract or other flavorings.
4. Gradually add the flour and salt (if using unsalted butter) to the butter-sugar mixture, mixing until a dough forms. The dough should come together and be slightly crumbly but hold its shape when pressed.
5. Gather the dough into a ball and flatten it into a disk. Wrap the dough in plastic wrap and refrigerate for at least 30 minutes, or until firm.
6. On a lightly floured surface, roll out the chilled dough to about 1/4 inch thickness.
7. Use cookie cutters to cut out shapes or simply slice the dough into squares or rectangles using a knife.
8. Place the cookies on the prepared baking sheet, spacing them about 1 inch apart.
9. Prick the tops of the cookies with a fork to create a decorative pattern (optional).
10. Bake in the preheated oven for 12-15 minutes, or until the edges are lightly golden brown.
11. Remove from the oven and let the cookies cool on the baking sheet for a few minutes before transferring them to a wire rack to cool completely.
12. Enjoy your homemade shortbread cookies! These cookies are delicious on their own or dipped in chocolate or decorated with icing.

Store the cooled cookies in an airtight container at room temperature for up to one week. They also freeze well for longer storage.

Cinnamon Rolls

Ingredients:

For the Dough:

- 1 cup warm milk (about 110°F)
- 2 1/4 teaspoons (1 packet) active dry yeast
- 1/2 cup granulated sugar
- 1/3 cup unsalted butter, melted
- 2 large eggs, room temperature
- 1 teaspoon salt
- 4 1/2 cups all-purpose flour

For the Filling:

- 1 cup packed light brown sugar
- 2 1/2 tablespoons ground cinnamon
- 1/3 cup unsalted butter, softened

For the Cream Cheese Icing:

- 4 oz cream cheese, softened
- 1/4 cup unsalted butter, softened
- 1 cup powdered sugar
- 1/2 teaspoon vanilla extract

Instructions:

1. **Activate the Yeast:**
   - In a small bowl, combine the warm milk and yeast. Let it sit for 5-10 minutes until frothy.
2. **Prepare the Dough:**
   - In a large bowl or the bowl of a stand mixer fitted with the dough hook attachment, combine the yeast mixture with the melted butter, sugar, eggs, and salt.
   - Gradually add the flour, 1 cup at a time, mixing until a soft dough forms. The dough should be slightly sticky but manageable. You may not need to use all of the flour.
   - Knead the dough for 5-7 minutes until smooth and elastic. If using a stand mixer, knead on medium speed.
3. **First Rise:**
   - Place the dough in a greased bowl and cover it with a clean kitchen towel or plastic wrap.
   - Let the dough rise in a warm place for 1-1.5 hours, or until doubled in size.
4. **Prepare the Filling:**

- In a small bowl, mix together the brown sugar and cinnamon for the filling.
- Once the dough has risen, punch it down and roll it out on a lightly floured surface into a large rectangle, about 16x12 inches.

5. **Assemble the Cinnamon Rolls:**
   - Spread the softened butter evenly over the rolled-out dough.
   - Sprinkle the cinnamon-sugar mixture evenly over the butter.
6. **Roll and Cut the Rolls:**
   - Starting from one long edge, tightly roll up the dough into a log.
   - Cut the log into 12 even slices using a sharp knife or unflavored dental floss (slide under the log, cross over the top, and pull to slice).
7. **Second Rise:**
   - Place the cinnamon rolls in a greased 9x13-inch baking pan or two 9-inch round cake pans.
   - Cover the rolls loosely with a kitchen towel and let them rise in a warm place for 30-45 minutes, or until puffy and nearly doubled in size.
8. **Bake the Cinnamon Rolls:**
   - Preheat your oven to 350°F (175°C).
   - Bake the cinnamon rolls in the preheated oven for 20-25 minutes, or until golden brown on top and cooked through.
9. **Make the Cream Cheese Icing:**
   - While the rolls are baking, prepare the cream cheese icing. In a medium bowl, beat together the softened cream cheese and butter until smooth and creamy.
   - Add the powdered sugar and vanilla extract, and beat until smooth and fluffy.
10. **Ice and Serve:**
    - Remove the cinnamon rolls from the oven and let them cool in the pan for 5-10 minutes.
    - Spread the cream cheese icing evenly over the warm rolls.
    - Serve the cinnamon rolls warm and enjoy!

These homemade cinnamon rolls are best enjoyed fresh on the day they are baked. Store any leftovers covered at room temperature for up to 2 days, or in the refrigerator for longer storage. Reheat briefly in the microwave before serving if desired.

Cheesecake

Ingredients:

For the Crust:

- 1 1/2 cups graham cracker crumbs (about 12-14 graham crackers)
- 1/4 cup granulated sugar
- 1/2 cup unsalted butter, melted

For the Cheesecake Filling:

- 4 packages (8 oz each) cream cheese, softened
- 1 1/4 cups granulated sugar
- 4 large eggs, room temperature
- 1 cup sour cream, room temperature
- 1 tablespoon all-purpose flour
- 1 tablespoon vanilla extract
- 1/4 cup heavy cream

Instructions:

1. **Preheat your oven to 325°F (160°C).** Wrap the outside of a 9-inch springform pan with aluminum foil to prevent water from seeping into the pan during baking.
2. **Make the Crust:**
    - In a medium bowl, mix together the graham cracker crumbs, sugar, and melted butter until well combined.
    - Press the mixture evenly into the bottom of the prepared springform pan.
    - Bake the crust in the preheated oven for 10 minutes. Remove and set aside to cool while you prepare the filling.
3. **Prepare the Cheesecake Filling:**
    - In a large bowl or the bowl of a stand mixer fitted with the paddle attachment, beat the softened cream cheese and granulated sugar until smooth and creamy.
    - Add the eggs one at a time, mixing well after each addition.
    - Add the sour cream, flour, and vanilla extract, and beat until smooth and combined.
    - Finally, add the heavy cream and mix until incorporated.
4. **Assemble and Bake:**
    - Pour the cheesecake filling over the baked crust in the springform pan.
    - Tap the pan gently on the counter to remove any air bubbles.
    - Place the springform pan into a larger baking dish or roasting pan. Fill the larger pan with hot water halfway up the sides of the springform pan, creating a water bath.
5. **Bake the Cheesecake:**

- Bake in the preheated oven for 1 hour to 1 hour 15 minutes, or until the edges are set and the center is slightly jiggly.
- Turn off the oven and leave the cheesecake in the oven with the door slightly ajar for 1 hour to cool gradually.

6. **Chill the Cheesecake:**
    - Remove the cheesecake from the oven and water bath. Carefully run a knife around the edge of the pan to loosen the cheesecake from the sides.
    - Let the cheesecake cool completely at room temperature, then refrigerate for at least 4 hours or overnight until well chilled and set.

7. **Serve the Cheesecake:**
    - Before serving, remove the cheesecake from the springform pan.
    - Slice and serve chilled, optionally garnished with fresh berries, whipped cream, or a fruit compote.

Enjoy your homemade New York-style cheesecake! It's a perfect dessert for special occasions or anytime you crave a luxurious treat.

Scones

Ingredients:

- 2 cups all-purpose flour
- 1/4 cup granulated sugar
- 1 tablespoon baking powder
- 1/2 teaspoon salt
- 1/2 cup unsalted butter, cold and cut into small cubes
- 1/2 cup milk or buttermilk
- 1 large egg
- 1 teaspoon vanilla extract (optional)
- Optional add-ins: 1/2 cup dried fruit (such as raisins or cranberries), chocolate chips, nuts, or citrus zest

Instructions:

1. **Preheat your oven to 400°F (200°C).** Line a baking sheet with parchment paper or lightly grease it.
2. **Prepare the Dry Ingredients:**
   - In a large bowl, whisk together the flour, sugar, baking powder, and salt until well combined.
3. **Cut in the Butter:**
   - Add the cold butter cubes to the dry ingredients. Use a pastry cutter, two knives, or your fingertips to quickly work the butter into the flour mixture until it resembles coarse crumbs with some pea-sized pieces of butter remaining.
4. **Mix the Wet Ingredients:**
   - In a separate bowl, whisk together the milk (or buttermilk), egg, and vanilla extract (if using).
5. **Combine Wet and Dry Ingredients:**
   - Pour the wet ingredients into the dry ingredients. Mix gently with a fork or a spatula until the dough just starts to come together. Do not overmix.
6. **Add Optional Add-Ins:**
   - If using any optional add-ins like dried fruit, chocolate chips, nuts, or citrus zest, gently fold them into the dough until evenly distributed.
7. **Shape the Scones:**
   - Transfer the dough onto a lightly floured surface. Pat it into a circle about 1 inch thick.
8. **Cut the Dough:**
   - Use a sharp knife or a pastry cutter to cut the dough into wedges or use a round cutter to cut out circles.
9. **Bake the Scones:**
   - Place the scones on the prepared baking sheet, spacing them about 1 inch apart.
   - Optionally, brush the tops of the scones with a little milk or beaten egg for a golden finish.

10. **Bake in the preheated oven for 12-15 minutes,** or until the scones are lightly golden brown on top and cooked through.
11. **Cool and Serve:**
    - Remove the scones from the oven and let them cool on a wire rack for a few minutes before serving.
12. **Enjoy your homemade scones!** Serve warm with clotted cream, jam, or simply enjoy them plain.

These scones are best enjoyed fresh on the day they are baked. Store any leftovers in an airtight container at room temperature for up to 2 days, or freeze them for longer storage. Reheat briefly in the oven or microwave before serving if desired.

Chocolate Cake

Ingredients:

For the Cake:

- 1 and 3/4 cups all-purpose flour
- 1 and 1/2 cups granulated sugar
- 3/4 cup unsweetened cocoa powder
- 1 and 1/2 teaspoons baking powder
- 1 and 1/2 teaspoons baking soda
- 1 teaspoon salt
- 2 large eggs, at room temperature
- 1 cup whole milk, at room temperature
- 1/2 cup vegetable oil
- 2 teaspoons vanilla extract
- 1 cup boiling water

For the Chocolate Frosting:

- 1 cup unsalted butter, softened
- 3 and 1/2 cups powdered sugar
- 1/2 cup unsweetened cocoa powder
- 1/2 teaspoon salt
- 2 teaspoons vanilla extract
- 1/3 cup whole milk or heavy cream

Instructions:

1. **Preheat your oven to 350°F (175°C).** Grease and flour two 9-inch round cake pans or line them with parchment paper.
2. **Make the Cake:**
    - In a large bowl, sift together the flour, sugar, cocoa powder, baking powder, baking soda, and salt until well combined.
    - Add the eggs, milk, vegetable oil, and vanilla extract to the dry ingredients. Beat on medium speed with a hand mixer or in a stand mixer for about 2 minutes until well combined.
    - Stir in the boiling water. The batter will be thin; this is normal.
3. **Bake the Cake:**
    - Pour the batter evenly into the prepared cake pans.
    - Bake in the preheated oven for 30-35 minutes, or until a toothpick inserted into the center of the cakes comes out clean.
    - Remove from the oven and let the cakes cool in the pans for 10 minutes. Then, remove the cakes from the pans and transfer them to a wire rack to cool completely.

4. **Make the Chocolate Frosting:**
    - In a large bowl, beat the softened butter until smooth and creamy.
    - Add the powdered sugar, cocoa powder, salt, vanilla extract, and milk or heavy cream. Beat on low speed until combined, then increase the speed to medium-high and beat for 2-3 minutes until frosting is smooth and fluffy.
5. **Assemble the Cake:**
    - Place one cake layer on a serving plate or cake stand.
    - Spread a thick layer of chocolate frosting evenly over the top.
    - Place the second cake layer on top and frost the top and sides of the cake with the remaining frosting.
6. **Decorate (optional):**
    - Decorate the cake with chocolate shavings, sprinkles, or additional frosting decorations if desired.
7. **Serve and Enjoy!**
    - Slice and serve your homemade chocolate cake at room temperature. It's delicious on its own or with a scoop of vanilla ice cream.

Store any leftover cake covered at room temperature for up to 3 days, or in the refrigerator for longer storage. Allow the refrigerated cake to come to room temperature before serving for the best taste and texture.

Peanut Butter Cookies

Ingredients:

- 1/2 cup unsalted butter, softened
- 1/2 cup granulated sugar
- 1/2 cup packed light brown sugar
- 1/2 cup creamy peanut butter
- 1 large egg
- 1 teaspoon vanilla extract
- 1 and 1/4 cups all-purpose flour
- 1/2 teaspoon baking powder
- 1/2 teaspoon baking soda
- 1/4 teaspoon salt
- Additional granulated sugar for rolling (optional)

Instructions:

1. **Preheat your oven to 350°F (175°C).** Line a baking sheet with parchment paper or lightly grease it.
2. **Cream the Butter and Sugars:**
    - In a large bowl, cream together the softened butter, granulated sugar, and brown sugar until smooth and creamy.
3. **Add Peanut Butter and Wet Ingredients:**
    - Mix in the creamy peanut butter until well combined.
    - Add the egg and vanilla extract, and beat until smooth.
4. **Combine Dry Ingredients:**
    - In a separate bowl, whisk together the flour, baking powder, baking soda, and salt.
5. **Mix Wet and Dry Ingredients:**
    - Gradually add the dry ingredients to the wet ingredients, mixing until just combined. Do not overmix.
6. **Shape the Cookies:**
    - Roll the dough into 1-inch balls (about 1 tablespoon of dough each). Optionally, roll each ball in granulated sugar for a sparkly finish and extra crispness.
7. **Place on Baking Sheet:**
    - Arrange the balls on the prepared baking sheet, spacing them about 2 inches apart.
8. **Flatten with Fork (Optional):**
    - Use a fork to gently flatten each ball of dough, creating a crisscross pattern.
9. **Bake the Cookies:**
    - Bake in the preheated oven for 10-12 minutes, or until the cookies are lightly golden brown around the edges.
    - Remove from the oven and let the cookies cool on the baking sheet for 5 minutes before transferring them to a wire rack to cool completely.

10. **Enjoy your homemade peanut butter cookies!** Store any leftover cookies in an airtight container at room temperature for up to 1 week.

These cookies are perfect for enjoying with a glass of milk or sharing with friends and family. They also make wonderful gifts during the holiday season or any time of year!

Strawberry Shortcake

Ingredients:

For the Biscuits:

- 2 cups all-purpose flour
- 1/4 cup granulated sugar
- 1 tablespoon baking powder
- 1/2 teaspoon salt
- 1/2 cup unsalted butter, cold and cut into small cubes
- 3/4 cup milk (whole milk is preferred)
- 1 teaspoon vanilla extract (optional)
- 1 tablespoon heavy cream or milk, for brushing

For the Strawberries:

- 1 pound fresh strawberries, hulled and sliced
- 2-3 tablespoons granulated sugar (adjust to taste)
- 1 teaspoon vanilla extract (optional)

For the Whipped Cream:

- 1 cup heavy cream, chilled
- 2 tablespoons powdered sugar
- 1/2 teaspoon vanilla extract

Instructions:

1. **Make the Biscuits:**
    - Preheat your oven to 425°F (220°C). Line a baking sheet with parchment paper or lightly grease it.
    - In a large bowl, whisk together the flour, sugar, baking powder, and salt until well combined.
    - Add the cold butter cubes to the flour mixture. Use a pastry cutter, two knives, or your fingertips to quickly work the butter into the flour until it resembles coarse crumbs.
    - In a separate bowl, mix together the milk and vanilla extract (if using). Gradually add the milk mixture to the flour mixture, stirring until the dough just starts to come together.
    - Turn the dough out onto a lightly floured surface. Gently knead the dough a few times until it holds together.
    - Pat the dough into a circle about 1 inch thick. Use a round biscuit cutter or a glass to cut out biscuits, rerolling the scraps as needed.
    - Place the biscuits on the prepared baking sheet. Brush the tops with heavy cream or milk.

- Bake in the preheated oven for 12-15 minutes, or until the biscuits are golden brown on top. Remove from the oven and let them cool slightly on a wire rack.
2. **Prepare the Strawberries:**
    - In a medium bowl, toss the sliced strawberries with granulated sugar and vanilla extract (if using). Adjust the amount of sugar based on the sweetness of your strawberries. Let the strawberries sit for at least 15-20 minutes to macerate, releasing their juices.
3. **Make the Whipped Cream:**
    - In a chilled bowl, whip the heavy cream until it starts to thicken.
    - Add the powdered sugar and vanilla extract. Continue to whip until soft peaks form. Be careful not to overwhip.
4. **Assemble the Strawberry Shortcake:**
    - Slice the biscuits in half horizontally using a serrated knife.
    - Place the bottom half of a biscuit on a plate. Spoon a generous amount of strawberries and their juices over the biscuit.
    - Top with a dollop of whipped cream.
    - Place the other half of the biscuit on top, followed by more strawberries and whipped cream.
    - Serve immediately and enjoy your homemade strawberry shortcake!

Strawberry shortcake is best enjoyed fresh, but you can store the components separately (biscuits, strawberries, and whipped cream) and assemble just before serving if needed. It's a delightful dessert that celebrates the flavors of summer!

Oatmeal Raisin Cookies

Ingredients:

- 1 cup (2 sticks) unsalted butter, softened
- 1 cup packed light brown sugar
- 1/2 cup granulated sugar
- 2 large eggs
- 1 teaspoon vanilla extract
- 1 and 1/2 cups all-purpose flour
- 1 teaspoon baking soda
- 1 teaspoon ground cinnamon
- 1/2 teaspoon salt
- 3 cups old-fashioned rolled oats
- 1 cup raisins (or more, to taste)
- Optional: 1/2 cup chopped nuts (such as walnuts or pecans)

Instructions:

1. **Preheat your oven to 350°F (175°C).** Line a baking sheet with parchment paper or lightly grease it.
2. **Cream the Butter and Sugars:**
    - In a large bowl, cream together the softened butter, brown sugar, and granulated sugar until light and fluffy.
3. **Add Eggs and Vanilla:**
    - Add the eggs one at a time, mixing well after each addition.
    - Mix in the vanilla extract until well combined.
4. **Combine Dry Ingredients:**
    - In a separate bowl, whisk together the flour, baking soda, ground cinnamon, and salt.
5. **Mix Wet and Dry Ingredients:**
    - Gradually add the dry ingredients to the wet ingredients, mixing until just combined.
6. **Add Oats and Raisins:**
    - Stir in the rolled oats until evenly distributed in the dough.
    - Fold in the raisins (and chopped nuts, if using) until well incorporated.
7. **Chill the Dough (optional but recommended):**
    - For thicker cookies, chill the dough in the refrigerator for at least 30 minutes.
8. **Shape the Cookies:**
    - Drop tablespoon-sized balls of dough onto the prepared baking sheet, spacing them about 2 inches apart.
    - Optionally, flatten each ball slightly with the back of a spoon or your fingers for more uniform cookies.
9. **Bake the Cookies:**

- Bake in the preheated oven for 10-12 minutes, or until the edges are lightly golden brown.
10. **Cool and Enjoy:**
    - Remove the cookies from the oven and let them cool on the baking sheet for 5 minutes.
    - Transfer the cookies to a wire rack to cool completely.
11. **Store in an airtight container:** Enjoy your homemade oatmeal raisin cookies! These cookies are best stored in an airtight container at room temperature for up to 1 week. They also freeze well for longer storage.

These cookies are perfect for snacking, sharing, or enjoying with a glass of milk. The combination of oats, raisins, and cinnamon makes them a comforting treat for any occasion.

Pound Cake

Ingredients:

- 1 cup (2 sticks) unsalted butter, softened, plus extra for greasing the pan
- 1 and 1/2 cups granulated sugar
- 4 large eggs, at room temperature
- 2 cups all-purpose flour
- 1 teaspoon baking powder
- 1/2 teaspoon salt
- 1/2 cup whole milk, at room temperature
- 1 teaspoon vanilla extract

Instructions:

1. **Preheat your oven to 325°F (160°C)**. Grease a 9x5-inch loaf pan with butter and lightly dust with flour, tapping out any excess.
2. **Cream the Butter and Sugar:**
    - In a large bowl or the bowl of a stand mixer fitted with the paddle attachment, cream together the softened butter and granulated sugar until light and fluffy, about 5 minutes.
3. **Add Eggs:**
    - Add the eggs one at a time, beating well after each addition until fully incorporated.
4. **Combine Dry Ingredients:**
    - In a separate bowl, whisk together the flour, baking powder, and salt.
5. **Add Dry Ingredients and Milk:**
    - Gradually add the dry ingredients to the butter mixture, alternating with the milk, beginning and ending with the flour mixture. Mix until just combined after each addition. Do not overmix.
6. **Add Vanilla Extract:**
    - Stir in the vanilla extract until evenly distributed in the batter.
7. **Bake the Pound Cake:**
    - Pour the batter into the prepared loaf pan and smooth the top with a spatula.
    - Bake in the preheated oven for 60-70 minutes, or until a toothpick inserted into the center of the cake comes out clean or with just a few moist crumbs.
8. **Cool the Cake:**
    - Remove the pound cake from the oven and let it cool in the pan on a wire rack for 15-20 minutes.
9. **Remove from Pan:**
    - Carefully run a knife around the edges of the cake to loosen it from the pan, then invert the cake onto the wire rack to cool completely.
10. **Serve and Enjoy:**
    - Slice the pound cake and serve it plain, dusted with powdered sugar, or with a dollop of whipped cream and fresh berries.

Pound cake is delicious on its own or as a base for other desserts like trifles or strawberry shortcake. Store any leftover pound cake wrapped tightly in plastic wrap or in an airtight container at room temperature for up to 3 days, or in the refrigerator for longer storage. Enjoy this classic dessert!

Gingerbread Cookies

Ingredients:

For the Gingerbread Dough:

- 3 cups all-purpose flour
- 1 teaspoon baking soda
- 2 teaspoons ground ginger
- 1 and 1/2 teaspoons ground cinnamon
- 1/2 teaspoon ground cloves
- 1/2 teaspoon ground nutmeg
- 1/2 teaspoon salt
- 3/4 cup unsalted butter, softened
- 1/2 cup packed light brown sugar
- 1 large egg
- 1/2 cup unsulfured molasses
- 1 teaspoon vanilla extract

For the Royal Icing (optional):

- 2 cups powdered sugar
- 1 large egg white
- 1/2 teaspoon lemon juice or cream of tartar
- Food coloring (optional)

Instructions:

1. **Make the Gingerbread Dough:**
   - In a medium bowl, whisk together the flour, baking soda, ground ginger, cinnamon, cloves, nutmeg, and salt until well combined.
   - In a large bowl or the bowl of a stand mixer fitted with the paddle attachment, beat together the softened butter and brown sugar until light and fluffy.
   - Add the egg, molasses, and vanilla extract to the butter mixture. Beat until well combined.
   - Gradually add the flour mixture to the wet ingredients, mixing on low speed until a dough forms. If the dough is too sticky, add a bit more flour, 1 tablespoon at a time, until it is easier to handle.
   - Divide the dough in half, flatten each half into a disc, wrap in plastic wrap, and refrigerate for at least 1 hour or overnight.
2. **Roll and Cut the Cookies:**
   - Preheat your oven to 350°F (175°C). Line baking sheets with parchment paper.
   - On a lightly floured surface, roll out one disc of dough to about 1/4-inch thickness.

- Use gingerbread cookie cutters to cut out shapes. Place the cookies on the prepared baking sheets, spacing them about 1 inch apart.
- Gather and reroll scraps of dough as needed to cut out more cookies.
3. **Bake the Cookies:**
    - Bake the cookies in the preheated oven for 8-10 minutes, or until the edges are firm and just starting to brown.
    - Remove from the oven and let the cookies cool on the baking sheets for a few minutes before transferring them to wire racks to cool completely.
4. **Decorate with Royal Icing (optional):**
    - In a medium bowl, whisk together the powdered sugar, egg white, and lemon juice (or cream of tartar) until smooth and glossy.
    - If desired, divide the icing into separate bowls and add food coloring to create different colors.
    - Use a piping bag or small spoon to decorate the cooled gingerbread cookies with the royal icing. Let the icing set before storing or stacking the cookies.
5. **Enjoy your homemade gingerbread cookies!**
    - Store the cookies in an airtight container at room temperature for up to 1 week. They also freeze well for longer storage.

These gingerbread cookies are perfect for decorating with family and friends, and they make a wonderful holiday treat or edible gift. Adjust the spices and decorations to suit your taste and creativity!

Key Lime Pie

Ingredients:

For the Graham Cracker Crust:

- 1 and 1/2 cups graham cracker crumbs (about 10-12 whole graham crackers)
- 1/4 cup granulated sugar
- 6 tablespoons unsalted butter, melted

For the Key Lime Pie Filling:

- 4 large egg yolks
- 1 can (14 ounces) sweetened condensed milk
- 1/2 cup freshly squeezed key lime juice (regular lime juice can be used if key limes are not available)
- 1 tablespoon finely grated lime zest (from about 2-3 limes)

For Whipped Cream Topping (optional):

- 1 cup heavy cream, chilled
- 2 tablespoons powdered sugar
- 1/2 teaspoon vanilla extract

Instructions:

1. **Preheat your oven to 350°F (175°C).**
2. **Make the Graham Cracker Crust:**
    - In a medium bowl, combine the graham cracker crumbs, granulated sugar, and melted butter until well mixed.
    - Press the mixture firmly and evenly into the bottom and up the sides of a 9-inch pie dish.
    - Bake the crust in the preheated oven for 8-10 minutes, or until lightly golden brown. Remove from the oven and let it cool while you prepare the filling.
3. **Make the Key Lime Pie Filling:**
    - In a large bowl, whisk the egg yolks until smooth.
    - Gradually whisk in the sweetened condensed milk until well combined.
    - Whisk in the key lime juice and lime zest until smooth and slightly thickened.
    - Pour the filling into the cooled graham cracker crust.
4. **Bake the Pie:**
    - Bake the pie in the preheated oven for 15-18 minutes, or until the edges are set and the center is slightly jiggly.
    - Remove from the oven and let the pie cool to room temperature, then refrigerate for at least 2 hours (or overnight) to set.
5. **Prepare the Whipped Cream Topping (optional):**
    - In a chilled bowl, whip the heavy cream until it starts to thicken.

- Add the powdered sugar and vanilla extract, and continue whipping until soft peaks form.
- Spread or pipe the whipped cream over the chilled key lime pie before serving.
6. **Serve and Enjoy:**
    - Slice the key lime pie and serve chilled. Optionally, garnish each slice with additional lime zest or slices.

Key lime pie is best enjoyed cold, making it a perfect dessert for hot summer days or any time you crave a zesty, creamy treat. Store any leftover pie covered in the refrigerator for up to 3-4 days. Enjoy this classic dessert with its delightful balance of sweet and tart flavors!

Biscotti

Ingredients:

- 2 cups all-purpose flour
- 1 cup granulated sugar
- 1 teaspoon baking powder
- 1/4 teaspoon salt
- 3 large eggs
- 1 teaspoon vanilla extract
- 1 cup whole almonds, toasted and roughly chopped (or other add-ins like chocolate chips, dried fruits, etc.)

Instructions:

1. **Preheat your oven to 350°F (175°C).** Line a baking sheet with parchment paper or a silicone baking mat.
2. **Toast the Almonds (if not already toasted):**
   - Spread the almonds evenly on a baking sheet and toast in the preheated oven for about 8-10 minutes, or until lightly golden and fragrant. Let them cool, then roughly chop them.
3. **Mix Dry Ingredients:**
   - In a large bowl, whisk together the flour, sugar, baking powder, and salt until well combined.
4. **Combine Wet Ingredients:**
   - In a separate bowl, whisk together the eggs and vanilla extract until well blended.
5. **Form the Dough:**
   - Make a well in the center of the dry ingredients and pour in the egg mixture. Stir until the dough begins to come together.
   - Add the toasted almonds (or other add-ins) and knead gently until evenly distributed in the dough.
6. **Shape the Dough:**
   - Divide the dough in half. On a lightly floured surface, shape each half into a log about 12 inches long and 2 inches wide. Place the logs on the prepared baking sheet, spacing them a few inches apart.
7. **First Bake:**
   - Bake in the preheated oven for 25-30 minutes, or until the logs are firm to the touch and just beginning to crack on top. Remove from the oven and let cool on the baking sheet for about 10 minutes.
8. **Slice the Biscotti:**
   - Transfer the logs to a cutting board. Using a sharp serrated knife, slice the logs diagonally into 1/2-inch thick slices.
9. **Second Bake:**

- Arrange the biscotti cut-side down on the baking sheet. Bake for an additional 10-15 minutes, flipping the biscotti halfway through, until they are golden brown and crisp.
- Remove from the oven and let cool completely on a wire rack.

10. **Serve and Enjoy:**
    - Biscotti are best enjoyed dipped in coffee, tea, or dessert wine. Store them in an airtight container at room temperature for up to 2 weeks.

Feel free to customize your biscotti by adding different nuts, dried fruits, or even dipping them in chocolate after they've cooled for an extra indulgent treat. Enjoy these crunchy, flavorful cookies as a delightful snack or homemade gift!

Pecan Pie

Ingredients:

For the Pie Crust:

- 1 and 1/4 cups all-purpose flour
- 1/2 teaspoon salt
- 1/2 teaspoon granulated sugar
- 1/2 cup unsalted butter, cold and cut into cubes
- 2-4 tablespoons ice water

For the Pecan Pie Filling:

- 1 cup granulated sugar
- 3/4 cup light corn syrup
- 1/4 cup unsalted butter, melted
- 1 teaspoon vanilla extract
- 3 large eggs, lightly beaten
- 1 and 1/2 cups pecan halves

Instructions:

1. **Make the Pie Crust:**
    - In a large bowl, whisk together the flour, salt, and sugar.
    - Add the cold butter cubes to the flour mixture. Use a pastry cutter, two knives, or your fingertips to quickly work the butter into the flour until it resembles coarse crumbs.
    - Gradually add the ice water, 1 tablespoon at a time, mixing with a fork until the dough starts to come together.
    - Shape the dough into a disk, wrap it in plastic wrap, and refrigerate for at least 1 hour.
2. **Preheat your oven to 375°F (190°C).**
3. **Roll out the Pie Crust:**
    - On a lightly floured surface, roll out the chilled dough into a circle about 12 inches in diameter.
    - Transfer the rolled-out dough to a 9-inch pie dish. Trim any excess dough hanging over the edges and crimp the edges decoratively. Refrigerate while you prepare the filling.
4. **Make the Pecan Pie Filling:**
    - In a medium bowl, whisk together the granulated sugar, corn syrup, melted butter, and vanilla extract until well combined.
    - Add the lightly beaten eggs and whisk until smooth.
5. **Assemble and Bake the Pie:**
    - Arrange the pecan halves evenly over the bottom of the chilled pie crust.

- Pour the filling mixture over the pecans, making sure they are evenly coated.
6. **Bake the Pie:**
    - Place the pie in the preheated oven and bake for 40-50 minutes, or until the filling is set and slightly puffed, and the crust is golden brown.
7. **Cool and Serve:**
    - Remove the pie from the oven and let it cool completely on a wire rack before slicing and serving.
8. **Serve and Enjoy:**
    - Serve slices of pecan pie at room temperature or slightly warmed, optionally with a dollop of whipped cream or a scoop of vanilla ice cream.

Pecan pie is best enjoyed fresh on the day it's made, but leftovers can be stored covered in the refrigerator for up to 3 days. It's a beloved dessert that combines sweet, gooey filling with crunchy pecans, perfect for any celebration or gathering!

Coconut Macaroons

Ingredients:

- 3 cups sweetened shredded coconut
- 3/4 cup sweetened condensed milk
- 1 teaspoon vanilla extract
- 2 large egg whites
- 1/4 teaspoon salt

Optional Chocolate Drizzle:

- 1/2 cup semi-sweet or dark chocolate chips
- 1 teaspoon coconut oil or vegetable shortening (optional, for smoother chocolate)

Instructions:

1. **Preheat your oven to 325°F (160°C).** Line a baking sheet with parchment paper or a silicone baking mat.
2. **Mix the Ingredients:**
   - In a large bowl, combine the sweetened shredded coconut, sweetened condensed milk, and vanilla extract. Stir until well combined.
3. **Whip Egg Whites:**
   - In a separate bowl, using a hand mixer or stand mixer with the whisk attachment, beat the egg whites and salt until stiff peaks form.
4. **Combine and Fold:**
   - Gently fold the whipped egg whites into the coconut mixture until fully incorporated. Be careful not to deflate the egg whites too much.
5. **Form Macaroons:**
   - Using a spoon or cookie scoop, drop rounded tablespoons of the coconut mixture onto the prepared baking sheet, spacing them about 1 inch apart.
6. **Bake:**
   - Bake in the preheated oven for 18-20 minutes, or until the macaroons are lightly golden brown on the edges and set.
7. **Cool:**
   - Remove from the oven and let the macaroons cool on the baking sheet for a few minutes, then transfer them to a wire rack to cool completely.
8. **Optional Chocolate Drizzle:**
   - In a microwave-safe bowl, melt the chocolate chips and coconut oil or vegetable shortening in 30-second intervals, stirring in between, until smooth.
   - Drizzle the melted chocolate over the cooled macaroons using a spoon or by pouring the chocolate into a small zip-top bag and cutting off a tiny corner to pipe.
9. **Let Chocolate Set:**
   - Allow the chocolate drizzle to set at room temperature, or place the macaroons in the refrigerator for a quicker setting.

10. **Serve and Enjoy:**
    - Once the chocolate is set, serve and enjoy your homemade coconut macaroons! Store any leftovers in an airtight container at room temperature for up to 1 week.

These coconut macaroons are a wonderful treat for coconut lovers and make a great addition to dessert platters or cookie exchanges. They're also naturally gluten-free, making them suitable for those with dietary restrictions.

Raspberry Tart

Ingredients:

For the Tart Crust:

- 1 and 1/4 cups all-purpose flour
- 1/4 cup granulated sugar
- 1/4 teaspoon salt
- 1/2 cup unsalted butter, cold and cut into cubes
- 1 large egg yolk
- 1-2 tablespoons ice water

For the Raspberry Filling:

- 4 cups fresh raspberries, divided
- 1/2 cup granulated sugar
- 2 tablespoons cornstarch
- 1/4 cup water
- 1 tablespoon lemon juice
- Zest of 1 lemon

For the Glaze (optional):

- 1/4 cup seedless raspberry jam
- 1 tablespoon water

Instructions:

1. **Make the Tart Crust:**
    - In a food processor, pulse together the flour, sugar, and salt until combined.
    - Add the cold butter cubes and pulse until the mixture resembles coarse crumbs.
    - Add the egg yolk and pulse again until the dough starts to come together. If needed, add ice water, 1 tablespoon at a time, until the dough forms a ball.
    - Flatten the dough into a disk, wrap it in plastic wrap, and refrigerate for at least 30 minutes.
2. **Preheat your oven to 375°F (190°C).** Lightly grease a 9-inch tart pan with a removable bottom.
3. **Roll out the Tart Crust:**
    - On a lightly floured surface, roll out the chilled dough into a circle about 12 inches in diameter.
    - Carefully transfer the dough to the prepared tart pan, pressing it into the bottom and up the sides. Trim any excess dough hanging over the edges.
4. **Blind Bake the Crust:**
    - Line the tart crust with parchment paper or foil, and fill with pie weights, dried beans, or rice.

- Bake in the preheated oven for 15-20 minutes, or until the edges are lightly golden.
- Remove the parchment paper and weights, and continue baking for another 10-15 minutes, or until the crust is golden brown all over.
- Remove from the oven and let the crust cool completely on a wire rack.

5. **Make the Raspberry Filling:**
    - In a medium saucepan, combine 2 cups of raspberries, sugar, cornstarch, water, lemon juice, and lemon zest.
    - Cook over medium heat, stirring constantly, until the mixture comes to a boil and thickens.
    - Reduce the heat to low and simmer for 2-3 minutes, stirring continuously.
    - Remove from heat and let the raspberry filling cool slightly.
6. **Assemble the Raspberry Tart:**
    - Pour the warm raspberry filling into the cooled tart crust, spreading it evenly.
    - Arrange the remaining 2 cups of fresh raspberries on top of the filling.
7. **Optional Glaze:**
    - In a small saucepan, heat the raspberry jam and water over low heat until melted and smooth.
    - Brush the glaze over the top of the fresh raspberries for a shiny finish.
8. **Chill and Serve:**
    - Refrigerate the raspberry tart for at least 1-2 hours, or until the filling is set.
    - Slice and serve chilled, optionally garnished with whipped cream or a dusting of powdered sugar.

This raspberry tart is a wonderful dessert to serve on special occasions or during the summer when raspberries are in season. It combines a buttery crust with a vibrant raspberry filling that's both sweet and tart, making it a favorite among berry lovers. Enjoy the fresh flavors and elegant presentation of this delicious tart!

Coffee Cake

Ingredients:

For the Cake:

- 2 cups all-purpose flour
- 1 teaspoon baking powder
- 1 teaspoon baking soda
- 1/2 teaspoon salt
- 1/2 cup unsalted butter, softened
- 1 cup granulated sugar
- 2 large eggs
- 1 cup sour cream (or plain Greek yogurt)
- 1 teaspoon vanilla extract

For the Streusel Topping:

- 1/2 cup packed light brown sugar
- 1/2 cup all-purpose flour
- 1 teaspoon ground cinnamon
- 1/4 cup unsalted butter, melted

For the Glaze (optional):

- 1/2 cup powdered sugar
- 1-2 tablespoons milk or cream
- 1/2 teaspoon vanilla extract

Instructions:

1. **Preheat your oven to 350°F (175°C).** Grease and flour a 9x9-inch baking pan, or line it with parchment paper for easy removal.
2. **Make the Streusel Topping:**
   - In a medium bowl, combine the brown sugar, flour, and ground cinnamon.
   - Pour in the melted butter and stir until the mixture resembles coarse crumbs. Set aside.
3. **Make the Cake Batter:**
   - In a large bowl, whisk together the flour, baking powder, baking soda, and salt.
   - In another bowl or the bowl of a stand mixer, cream together the softened butter and granulated sugar until light and fluffy.
   - Add the eggs one at a time, beating well after each addition.
   - Mix in the sour cream (or yogurt) and vanilla extract until smooth and well combined.
4. **Assemble the Coffee Cake:**

- Spread half of the cake batter into the prepared baking pan, smoothing it out with a spatula.
- Sprinkle half of the streusel topping evenly over the batter.
- Carefully spread the remaining batter over the streusel layer.
- Top evenly with the remaining streusel mixture.

5. **Bake the Coffee Cake:**
    - Bake in the preheated oven for 35-40 minutes, or until a toothpick inserted into the center comes out clean or with a few moist crumbs.
6. **Make the Glaze (optional):**
    - In a small bowl, whisk together the powdered sugar, milk or cream, and vanilla extract until smooth.
    - Drizzle the glaze over the warm coffee cake after it has cooled for about 10-15 minutes.
7. **Serve and Enjoy:**
    - Allow the coffee cake to cool in the pan for at least 20-30 minutes before slicing and serving.
    - Serve slices of coffee cake warm or at room temperature, with a hot cup of coffee or tea.

This homemade coffee cake is perfect for breakfast, brunch, or as a comforting dessert. The combination of moist cake, cinnamon-spiced streusel, and optional glaze makes it irresistible and a favorite among family and friends.

Linzer Cookies

Ingredients:

For the Cookies:

- 1 cup unsalted butter, softened
- 2/3 cup granulated sugar
- 1 teaspoon vanilla extract
- 1 large egg
- 2 cups all-purpose flour
- 1/2 teaspoon ground cinnamon
- 1/4 teaspoon salt
- 3/4 cup ground almonds or almond flour

For Assembly:

- 1/2 cup raspberry or strawberry jam (or any jam of your choice)
- Powdered sugar, for dusting

Instructions:

1. **Prepare the Dough:**
    - In a large bowl or the bowl of a stand mixer, cream together the softened butter and granulated sugar until light and fluffy.
    - Add the vanilla extract and egg, and beat until well combined.
2. **Combine Dry Ingredients:**
    - In a separate bowl, whisk together the flour, ground cinnamon, salt, and ground almonds.
3. **Mix the Dough:**
    - Gradually add the dry ingredients to the butter mixture, mixing on low speed until a dough forms. If the dough seems too soft, refrigerate it for 30 minutes to 1 hour to firm up.
4. **Chill the Dough:**
    - Divide the dough in half. Flatten each half into a disk, wrap in plastic wrap, and refrigerate for at least 1 hour or until firm.
5. **Preheat your oven to 350°F (175°C).** Line baking sheets with parchment paper.
6. **Roll and Cut Out the Cookies:**
    - On a lightly floured surface, roll out one disk of chilled dough to about 1/8 inch thickness.
    - Use a round cookie cutter (about 2 inches in diameter) to cut out the cookies. Use a smaller cookie cutter to cut a small hole in the center of half of the cookies (these will be the top cookies).
7. **Bake the Cookies:**

- Place the cookies on the prepared baking sheets, spacing them about 1 inch apart.
- Bake in the preheated oven for 10-12 minutes, or until the edges are lightly golden.
- Remove from the oven and let the cookies cool on the baking sheets for a few minutes before transferring them to wire racks to cool completely.

8. **Assemble the Cookies:**
   - Spread about 1 teaspoon of jam onto the bottom (solid) cookies, leaving a small border around the edges.
   - Place a cut-out cookie on top of each jam-covered cookie, gently pressing down to sandwich them together.
9. **Dust with Powdered Sugar:**
   - Dust the tops of the assembled cookies with powdered sugar using a fine-mesh sieve.
10. **Serve and Enjoy:**
    - Arrange the Linzer cookies on a serving plate and enjoy their delightful flavor and appearance!

These Linzer cookies are not only delicious but also make a beautiful addition to holiday cookie platters or as a special treat for any occasion. The combination of buttery almond-flavored cookies and sweet jam filling is simply irresistible!

Eclairs

Ingredients:

For the Choux Pastry:

- 1/2 cup unsalted butter
- 1 cup water
- 1/4 teaspoon salt
- 1 cup all-purpose flour
- 4 large eggs

For the Pastry Cream:

- 1 and 1/2 cups whole milk
- 1/2 cup granulated sugar
- 4 large egg yolks
- 1/4 cup cornstarch
- 1 teaspoon vanilla extract
- Pinch of salt

For the Chocolate Glaze:

- 4 ounces semisweet or bittersweet chocolate, finely chopped
- 1/2 cup heavy cream
- 1 tablespoon unsalted butter

Instructions:

1. **Make the Choux Pastry:**
   - Preheat your oven to 400°F (200°C). Line a baking sheet with parchment paper or a silicone baking mat.
   - In a medium saucepan, combine the butter, water, and salt. Bring to a boil over medium-high heat.
   - Reduce the heat to low and add the flour all at once. Stir vigorously with a wooden spoon until the mixture forms a ball and pulls away from the sides of the pan.
   - Transfer the dough to a mixing bowl and let it cool for 5-10 minutes.
   - Add the eggs one at a time, beating well after each addition, until the dough is smooth and glossy.
2. **Pipe and Bake the Eclairs:**
   - Transfer the choux pastry dough to a pastry bag fitted with a large round tip (or a zip-top bag with a corner cut off).
   - Pipe 4-5 inch long strips onto the prepared baking sheet, spacing them about 2 inches apart.
   - Smooth out any peaks or imperfections with a wet finger.

- Bake in the preheated oven for 15 minutes, then reduce the oven temperature to 350°F (175°C) and bake for an additional 20-25 minutes, or until the eclairs are golden brown and puffed.
- Remove from the oven and let them cool completely on a wire rack.

3. **Make the Pastry Cream:**
   - In a medium saucepan, heat the milk over medium heat until steaming (do not boil).
   - In a separate bowl, whisk together the sugar, egg yolks, cornstarch, vanilla extract, and salt until smooth and pale.
   - Gradually pour the hot milk into the egg mixture, whisking constantly.
   - Return the mixture to the saucepan and cook over medium heat, whisking constantly, until thickened and smooth.
   - Remove from heat and transfer to a bowl. Press a piece of plastic wrap directly onto the surface of the pastry cream to prevent a skin from forming. Refrigerate until completely chilled.

4. **Fill the Eclairs:**
   - Once the eclairs and pastry cream are cooled, use a small knife to make a slit along one side of each eclair.
   - Spoon or pipe the chilled pastry cream into each eclair until filled.

5. **Make the Chocolate Glaze:**
   - Place the chopped chocolate in a heatproof bowl.
   - In a small saucepan, heat the cream until just simmering.
   - Pour the hot cream over the chopped chocolate and let it sit for 1-2 minutes.
   - Add the butter and stir until the chocolate is melted and the mixture is smooth and shiny.

6. **Glaze the Eclairs:**
   - Dip the tops of each filled eclair into the chocolate glaze, allowing any excess to drip off.
   - Place the glazed eclairs on a wire rack set over a baking sheet to catch drips. Let the glaze set at room temperature.

7. **Serve and Enjoy:**
   - Once the chocolate glaze has set, serve the eclairs immediately for the best texture and flavor.

Eclairs are best enjoyed fresh but can be stored in the refrigerator for up to 2 days. They make a stunning dessert for special occasions and are sure to impress with their light pastry, creamy filling, and decadent chocolate topping. Enjoy making these elegant French pastries at home!

Angel Food Cake

Ingredients:

- 1 cup cake flour (sifted before measuring)
- 1 and 1/2 cups granulated sugar, divided
- 12 large egg whites, room temperature
- 1 teaspoon cream of tartar
- 1/4 teaspoon salt
- 1 and 1/2 teaspoons vanilla extract
- 1/2 teaspoon almond extract (optional)

Instructions:

1. **Preheat your oven to 350°F (175°C).**
2. **Prepare the Cake Pan:**
   - Use a 10-inch angel food cake pan (tube pan) with a removable bottom. Do not grease the pan; the cake needs to cling to the sides as it rises.
3. **Sift the Flour and Sugar:**
   - Sift the cake flour and 1/2 cup of granulated sugar together three times to ensure it's well combined and aerated.
4. **Whip the Egg Whites:**
   - In a large bowl or the bowl of a stand mixer fitted with the whisk attachment, beat the egg whites on medium speed until foamy.
   - Add the cream of tartar and salt. Increase the speed to medium-high and continue beating until soft peaks form.
   - Gradually add the remaining 1 cup of granulated sugar, about 2 tablespoons at a time, while continuing to beat until stiff peaks form. The egg whites should be glossy and hold stiff peaks when the beaters are lifted.
5. **Fold in the Flour Mixture:**
   - Gently sift the flour mixture over the whipped egg whites in four additions, folding gently with a spatula after each addition until no streaks of flour remain.
   - Fold in the vanilla extract and almond extract (if using) until just combined.
6. **Transfer the Batter to the Pan:**
   - Carefully spoon the batter into the ungreased angel food cake pan, smoothing the top with a spatula.
7. **Bake the Cake:**
   - Bake in the preheated oven for 35-40 minutes, or until the top is golden brown and springs back when lightly touched.
   - The cake should also start to pull away from the sides of the pan.
8. **Cool the Cake:**
   - Immediately invert the cake pan onto a wire rack (or balance it on the neck of a bottle) to cool completely, about 1-2 hours.
   - This step helps prevent the cake from collapsing as it cools.
9. **Remove the Cake from the Pan:**

- Once completely cooled, run a knife around the edges of the pan and around the center tube to loosen the cake.
- Carefully lift the cake out of the pan by pulling the center tube. Use a knife to gently loosen the bottom of the cake from the pan.

10. **Serve and Enjoy:**
    - Slice the angel food cake with a serrated knife and serve plain or with fresh berries and whipped cream.

Angel food cake is best enjoyed fresh on the day it's made but can be stored in an airtight container at room temperature for up to 2 days. It's a delightful, light dessert that's perfect for any occasion, from birthdays to summer gatherings.

Focaccia Bread

Ingredients:

- 4 cups all-purpose flour
- 2 teaspoons salt
- 1 tablespoon granulated sugar
- 2 teaspoons instant yeast
- 2 cups lukewarm water
- 1/4 cup extra-virgin olive oil, plus more for drizzling
- Toppings (optional): coarse sea salt, fresh rosemary, cherry tomatoes, olives, etc.

Instructions:

1. **Mix the Dough:**
    - In a large bowl, whisk together the flour, salt, sugar, and instant yeast.
    - Make a well in the center and pour in the lukewarm water and olive oil.
    - Stir with a wooden spoon or your hands until a shaggy dough forms.
2. **Knead the Dough:**
    - Turn the dough out onto a lightly floured surface and knead for about 5-7 minutes, or until the dough is smooth and elastic.
    - Alternatively, you can knead the dough using a stand mixer fitted with a dough hook on medium speed for 5-7 minutes.
3. **First Rise:**
    - Form the dough into a ball and place it in a lightly oiled bowl, turning to coat the dough with oil.
    - Cover the bowl with plastic wrap or a clean kitchen towel and let the dough rise in a warm, draft-free place for 1-1.5 hours, or until doubled in size.
4. **Prepare the Pan:**
    - Lightly grease a 9x13-inch baking pan with olive oil.
5. **Shape the Focaccia:**
    - Gently punch down the dough to deflate it. Transfer it to the prepared baking pan.
    - Using your fingertips, press the dough evenly into the pan, stretching it out to fit. If the dough resists, let it rest for 5-10 minutes and then continue to press it out.
    - Cover the pan loosely with plastic wrap or a clean kitchen towel and let it rest for 15-20 minutes.
6. **Second Rise:**
    - Preheat your oven to 400°F (200°C) during this resting period.
    - After resting, uncover the dough. Using your fingertips, make deep dimples all over the surface of the dough.
7. **Add Toppings (Optional):**
    - Drizzle the top of the focaccia with more olive oil, allowing it to pool in the dimples.
    - Sprinkle with coarse sea salt and any other toppings you desire, such as fresh rosemary, cherry tomatoes, olives, or thinly sliced onions.

8. **Bake the Focaccia:**
   - Bake in the preheated oven for 20-25 minutes, or until the focaccia is golden brown on top and sounds hollow when tapped on the bottom.
   - If adding tomatoes or other delicate toppings, you may want to add them halfway through baking to prevent burning.
9. **Cool and Serve:**
   - Remove the focaccia from the oven and let it cool in the pan for 5 minutes.
   - Transfer to a wire rack to cool completely or serve warm.
10. **Enjoy:**
    - Slice the focaccia and enjoy it warm or at room temperature. It's delicious on its own, dipped in olive oil and balsamic vinegar, or used as a base for sandwiches.

Homemade focaccia is a wonderful treat that's perfect for sharing with friends and family. Its versatility and satisfying texture make it a favorite bread for many occasions.

Cheese Danish

Ingredients:

For the Dough:

- 2 and 1/4 cups all-purpose flour
- 1/4 cup granulated sugar
- 1/2 teaspoon salt
- 2 and 1/4 teaspoons instant yeast
- 1/2 cup unsalted butter, softened
- 1/4 cup milk, lukewarm
- 1/4 cup water, lukewarm
- 2 large eggs, room temperature

For the Cheese Filling:

- 8 ounces cream cheese, softened
- 1/4 cup granulated sugar
- 1 teaspoon vanilla extract
- 1 large egg yolk
- Zest of 1 lemon (optional)

For the Glaze (optional):

- 1/2 cup powdered sugar
- 1-2 tablespoons milk or cream
- 1/2 teaspoon vanilla extract

Instructions:

1. **Make the Dough:**
    - In a large bowl or the bowl of a stand mixer fitted with the dough hook, combine the flour, sugar, salt, and instant yeast.
    - Add the softened butter, lukewarm milk, lukewarm water, and eggs.
    - Mix on low speed until the dough starts to come together, then increase the speed to medium and knead for about 5-7 minutes, or until the dough is smooth and elastic.
2. **First Rise:**
    - Place the dough in a lightly oiled bowl, turning to coat the dough with oil.
    - Cover the bowl with plastic wrap or a clean kitchen towel and let the dough rise in a warm, draft-free place for about 1-1.5 hours, or until doubled in size.
3. **Make the Cheese Filling:**
    - In a medium bowl, beat together the softened cream cheese, sugar, vanilla extract, egg yolk, and lemon zest (if using) until smooth and creamy. Set aside.
4. **Assemble the Cheese Danish:**

- Once the dough has doubled in size, punch it down to deflate it and transfer it to a lightly floured surface.
- Roll out the dough into a large rectangle, about 12x18 inches.
- Cut the dough into 12 equal squares using a pizza cutter or sharp knife.

5. **Fill and Shape the Danish:**
   - Place a spoonful of the cheese filling (about 2 tablespoons) in the center of each dough square.
   - Fold two opposite corners of each square over the filling, overlapping slightly in the center.
   - Transfer the shaped danishes to parchment-lined baking sheets, spacing them apart.
6. **Second Rise:**
   - Cover the shaped danishes loosely with plastic wrap or a clean kitchen towel and let them rise in a warm place for about 30-45 minutes, or until slightly puffed.
7. **Preheat your oven to 375°F (190°C)** during the last 15 minutes of the second rise.
8. **Bake the Cheese Danish:**
   - Bake the danishes in the preheated oven for 15-18 minutes, or until golden brown and the cheese filling is set.
   - Remove from the oven and let cool on the baking sheets for a few minutes before transferring them to a wire rack to cool completely.
9. **Optional Glaze:**
   - In a small bowl, whisk together the powdered sugar, milk or cream, and vanilla extract until smooth.
   - Drizzle the glaze over the cooled danishes before serving.
10. **Serve and Enjoy:**
    - Serve the cheese danish warm or at room temperature. They are best enjoyed fresh but can be stored in an airtight container in the refrigerator for up to 3 days. Warm slightly before serving if refrigerated.

These homemade cheese danishes are sure to impress with their flaky pastry and creamy cheese filling. They make a delightful treat for breakfast, brunch, or dessert. Enjoy making and sharing these delicious pastries with family and friends!

Macarons

Ingredients:

For the Macaron Shells:

- 1 cup (100g) almond flour
- 1 and 3/4 cups (210g) powdered sugar
- 3 large egg whites (about 100g), at room temperature
- 1/4 cup (50g) granulated sugar
- Gel food coloring (optional)

For the Filling:

- 1/2 cup (115g) unsalted butter, softened
- 1 cup (120g) powdered sugar
- 1-2 tablespoons heavy cream
- 1 teaspoon vanilla extract
- Jam, ganache, or curd for filling (optional)

Instructions:

1. **Prepare Baking Sheets:**
   - Line two baking sheets with parchment paper or silicone mats. If using parchment paper, you can trace circles using a round cookie cutter or the bottom of a glass to guide your piping.
2. **Make the Macaron Batter:**
   - In a food processor, pulse together the almond flour and powdered sugar until well combined and fine. Sift the mixture into a large bowl to remove any lumps.
   - In a separate bowl, beat the egg whites with a hand mixer or stand mixer until foamy. Gradually add the granulated sugar, a spoonful at a time, while continuing to beat. Add gel food coloring, if using, to achieve desired color.
   - Continue beating until stiff peaks form. The meringue should be glossy and hold its shape when the beaters are lifted.
   - Gently fold the almond flour mixture into the meringue in three additions, using a spatula. The batter should be smooth and flowing, but not too runny.
3. **Pipe the Macarons:**
   - Transfer the batter to a piping bag fitted with a round tip (usually about 1/2 inch in diameter).
   - Pipe rounds of batter onto the prepared baking sheets, spacing them about 1 inch apart. You can use the traced circles as a guide, piping just inside the lines.
   - Tap the baking sheets firmly on the counter a few times to release any air bubbles. This helps prevent cracking during baking.
4. **Rest and Preheat:**

- Let the piped macarons sit at room temperature for about 30 minutes to 1 hour. This allows them to develop a skin on the surface, which helps create the characteristic feet.
- Preheat your oven to 325°F (160°C) during this resting period.

5. **Bake the Macarons:**
    - Bake the macarons, one sheet at a time, in the preheated oven for 12-15 minutes, or until the macarons are set and just barely starting to brown.
    - Remove from the oven and let cool completely on the baking sheets.
6. **Make the Filling:**
    - While the macarons are cooling, prepare the filling. In a bowl, beat the softened butter until creamy.
    - Gradually add the powdered sugar, beating until smooth and fluffy. Add the heavy cream and vanilla extract, and beat until well combined and creamy.
7. **Assemble the Macarons:**
    - Match up the cooled macaron shells by size and shape.
    - Pipe or spoon a small amount of filling onto the flat side of one shell. If desired, add a small dollop of jam, ganache, or curd on top of the filling.
    - Gently sandwich together with another shell, pressing down lightly to spread the filling to the edges.
8. **Store and Enjoy:**
    - Place the assembled macarons in an airtight container and refrigerate for 24 hours before serving. This allows the flavors to meld and the texture to mature.
    - Bring to room temperature before serving for the best flavor and texture.

Macarons are delicate and elegant treats that can be customized with various flavors and colors. With practice, you can perfect your technique and create beautiful homemade macarons that rival those from a bakery. Enjoy the process and savor the delicious results!

Rugelach

Ingredients:

For the Dough:

- 1 cup (225g) unsalted butter, softened
- 1 package (8 oz or 225g) cream cheese, softened
- 1/4 cup (50g) granulated sugar
- 1/4 teaspoon salt
- 2 cups (250g) all-purpose flour

For the Filling:

- 1/2 cup (100g) packed brown sugar
- 1 tablespoon ground cinnamon
- 1 cup (120g) finely chopped nuts (walnuts, pecans, or almonds)
- 1/2 cup (80g) raisins or chopped dried fruit
- Jam or preserves (optional, for spreading on dough before adding filling)

For Finishing:

- 1 egg, beaten (for egg wash)
- Granulated sugar, for sprinkling

Instructions:

1. **Make the Dough:**
    - In a large bowl or the bowl of a stand mixer fitted with the paddle attachment, beat together the softened butter, cream cheese, granulated sugar, and salt until smooth and creamy.
    - Gradually add the flour, mixing until the dough comes together and forms a ball.
    - Divide the dough into 4 equal portions, flatten each portion into a disk, wrap tightly in plastic wrap, and refrigerate for at least 1 hour or overnight.
2. **Prepare the Filling:**
    - In a medium bowl, combine the brown sugar, ground cinnamon, chopped nuts, and raisins or dried fruit. Mix well until evenly combined. Set aside.
3. **Assemble the Rugelach:**
    - Preheat your oven to 350°F (175°C). Line baking sheets with parchment paper.
    - Take one portion of the chilled dough out of the refrigerator. On a lightly floured surface, roll out the dough into a circle about 1/8 inch thick.
    - If desired, spread a thin layer of jam or preserves over the dough to add extra flavor (optional).
    - Sprinkle a quarter of the filling mixture evenly over the rolled-out dough, pressing it lightly into the dough.

- Using a pizza cutter or sharp knife, cut the dough into 12 wedges (like slicing a pizza).
- Starting at the wide end, roll each wedge up tightly to form a crescent shape. Place each rugelach on the prepared baking sheets, seam side down.

4. **Bake the Rugelach:**
   - Brush each rugelach with beaten egg, then sprinkle with granulated sugar.
   - Bake in the preheated oven for 20-25 minutes, or until golden brown and crispy.

5. **Cool and Serve:**
   - Remove the rugelach from the oven and let them cool on the baking sheets for a few minutes before transferring them to wire racks to cool completely.
   - Enjoy these delicious rugelach at room temperature. They can be stored in an airtight container at room temperature for several days, although they are best enjoyed fresh.

Rugelach are perfect for holidays, brunches, or any occasion where you want to serve a delicious homemade pastry. The combination of flaky cream cheese dough and sweet, nutty filling makes them irresistible!

Baklava

Ingredients:

For the Baklava:

- 1 package (16 oz) phyllo dough, thawed if frozen
- 1 and 1/2 cups unsalted butter, melted
- 2 cups chopped nuts (such as walnuts, pistachios, or a mix)
- 1/2 cup granulated sugar
- 1 teaspoon ground cinnamon
- 1/4 teaspoon ground cloves (optional)

For the Syrup:

- 1 cup water
- 1 cup granulated sugar
- 1/2 cup honey
- 1 cinnamon stick
- 1 strip of lemon peel

Instructions:

1. **Prepare the Syrup:**
   - In a saucepan, combine water, sugar, honey, cinnamon stick, and lemon peel. Bring to a boil over medium-high heat, stirring occasionally until sugar is dissolved.
   - Reduce heat to low and simmer for about 10-15 minutes, until the syrup slightly thickens. Remove from heat and let cool completely. Once cooled, discard the cinnamon stick and lemon peel.
2. **Prepare the Baklava Filling:**
   - In a bowl, combine chopped nuts, granulated sugar, ground cinnamon, and ground cloves (if using). Mix well and set aside.
3. **Assemble the Baklava:**
   - Preheat your oven to 350°F (175°C). Lightly grease a 9x13-inch baking dish.
   - Unroll the phyllo dough and cover it with a damp towel to keep it from drying out.
   - Place one sheet of phyllo dough into the prepared baking dish and brush it generously with melted butter. Repeat with 7 more sheets, brushing each with butter.
   - Sprinkle a thin layer of the nut mixture (about 1/3 cup) evenly over the buttered phyllo layer.
   - Continue layering phyllo sheets and butter, sprinkling nuts between every 2-3 layers, until all nuts are used (about 4-5 layers of nuts).
   - Top with 8-10 layers of phyllo dough, brushing each with butter. Brush the top layer generously with butter.

4. **Cut and Bake the Baklava:**
   - Using a sharp knife, carefully cut the baklava into diamond or square shapes, cutting all the way through the layers.
   - Bake in the preheated oven for 45-50 minutes, or until golden brown and crisp.
5. **Add Syrup:**
   - Remove the baklava from the oven and immediately pour the cooled syrup evenly over the hot baklava. Let it cool completely in the pan to allow the syrup to soak in.
6. **Serve:**
   - Once cooled, carefully lift the pieces of baklava out of the baking dish and arrange them on a serving platter. Serve at room temperature.
7. **Enjoy:**
   - Baklava can be stored at room temperature, covered with foil or in an airtight container, for up to a week. The flavors develop even more over time.

Baklava is a wonderful treat with its crispy layers of phyllo, sweet and nutty filling, and fragrant syrup. It's perfect for holidays, celebrations, or any time you want to indulge in a decadent dessert!

Lemon Poppy Seed Muffins

Ingredients:

- 2 cups all-purpose flour
- 3/4 cup granulated sugar
- 2 teaspoons baking powder
- 1/2 teaspoon baking soda
- 1/4 teaspoon salt
- Zest of 2 lemons
- 1/2 cup unsalted butter, melted and cooled
- 1 cup plain yogurt or sour cream
- 2 large eggs
- 1/4 cup fresh lemon juice
- 1 teaspoon vanilla extract
- 2 tablespoons poppy seeds

For the Glaze (optional):

- 1/2 cup powdered sugar
- 1-2 tablespoons fresh lemon juice

Instructions:

1. Preheat your oven to 375°F (190°C). Line a muffin tin with paper liners or grease with non-stick cooking spray.
2. In a large bowl, whisk together the flour, sugar, baking powder, baking soda, salt, and lemon zest.
3. In another bowl, whisk together the melted butter, yogurt (or sour cream), eggs, lemon juice, and vanilla extract until smooth.
4. Pour the wet ingredients into the dry ingredients and gently fold together with a spatula until just combined. Be careful not to overmix; the batter should be lumpy.
5. Add the poppy seeds to the batter and fold gently to distribute evenly.
6. Spoon the batter into the prepared muffin tin, filling each cup about 3/4 full.
7. Bake for 15-18 minutes, or until a toothpick inserted into the center of a muffin comes out clean or with a few moist crumbs.
8. While the muffins are baking, prepare the optional glaze: In a small bowl, whisk together the powdered sugar and lemon juice until smooth. Adjust consistency by adding more sugar or juice as needed.
9. Once baked, remove the muffins from the oven and let them cool in the tin for 5 minutes before transferring to a wire rack to cool completely.
10. If desired, drizzle the glaze over the cooled muffins. Allow the glaze to set before serving.

These lemon poppy seed muffins are best enjoyed fresh but can be stored in an airtight container at room temperature for up to 3 days. They make a wonderful breakfast or snack, perfect with a cup of tea or coffee. Enjoy baking and indulging in these flavorful treats!

Almond Biscotti

Ingredients:

- 2 cups (250g) all-purpose flour
- 1 and 1/2 teaspoons baking powder
- 1/4 teaspoon salt
- 3/4 cup (150g) granulated sugar
- 1/2 cup (115g) unsalted butter, softened
- 2 large eggs
- 1 teaspoon vanilla extract
- 1 cup (120g) whole almonds, toasted and coarsely chopped

For brushing:

- 1 egg white
- 1 tablespoon water

Instructions:

1. Preheat your oven to 350°F (175°C). Line a baking sheet with parchment paper.
2. In a medium bowl, whisk together the flour, baking powder, and salt. Set aside.
3. In a large bowl or the bowl of a stand mixer, beat together the softened butter and granulated sugar until light and fluffy.
4. Add the eggs one at a time, beating well after each addition. Stir in the vanilla extract.
5. Gradually add the flour mixture to the wet ingredients, mixing until just combined. Fold in the chopped almonds.
6. Divide the dough in half. With lightly floured hands, shape each half into a log about 12 inches long and 2 inches wide on the prepared baking sheet.
7. In a small bowl, whisk together the egg white and water. Brush the tops and sides of the logs with the egg wash.
8. Bake in the preheated oven for 25-30 minutes, or until the logs are firm and lightly golden.
9. Remove from the oven and let cool on the baking sheet for 10-15 minutes. Reduce the oven temperature to 325°F (160°C).
10. Transfer the logs to a cutting board and slice diagonally into 1/2-inch thick slices using a serrated knife.
11. Place the slices cut-side down on the baking sheet.
12. Bake for an additional 10-15 minutes, flipping the biscotti halfway through baking, until the biscotti are golden and crisp.
13. Remove from the oven and let cool completely on wire racks.
14. Once cooled, store the almond biscotti in an airtight container at room temperature.

Enjoy these almond biscotti with your favorite hot beverage or as a sweet treat any time of the day. They also make wonderful gifts when packaged beautifully!

Fruitcake

Ingredients:

- 1 cup (225g) unsalted butter, softened
- 1 cup (200g) granulated sugar
- 4 large eggs
- 1/4 cup (60ml) brandy, rum, or orange juice (for soaking fruits)
- 2 cups (300g) mixed dried fruits (such as raisins, currants, chopped apricots, chopped dates, candied cherries, etc.)
- 1 cup (150g) mixed nuts (such as walnuts, pecans, almonds), chopped
- 2 cups (250g) all-purpose flour
- 1 teaspoon baking powder
- 1/2 teaspoon salt
- 1 teaspoon ground cinnamon
- 1/2 teaspoon ground nutmeg
- 1/4 teaspoon ground cloves
- 1/4 teaspoon ground allspice
- Zest of 1 lemon and 1 orange
- 1/2 cup (120ml) milk

For soaking the baked fruitcake:

- 1/4 cup (60ml) brandy, rum, or orange juice

Instructions:

1. **Prepare the Fruits:**
    - In a bowl, combine the mixed dried fruits with 1/4 cup of brandy, rum, or orange juice. Cover and let them soak for at least 1 hour, or overnight, stirring occasionally.
2. **Preheat your oven to 325°F (160°C). Grease and flour a 9x5-inch loaf pan or line it with parchment paper.**
3. **Make the Fruitcake Batter:**
    - In a large bowl, cream together the softened butter and granulated sugar until light and fluffy.
    - Add the eggs one at a time, beating well after each addition.
    - In a separate bowl, whisk together the flour, baking powder, salt, cinnamon, nutmeg, cloves, and allspice.
    - Gradually add the dry ingredients to the butter mixture, alternating with the milk, beginning and ending with the flour mixture. Mix until just combined.
    - Fold in the soaked dried fruits (including any liquid), chopped nuts, lemon zest, and orange zest until evenly distributed.
4. **Bake the Fruitcake:**
    - Pour the batter into the prepared loaf pan, smoothing the top with a spatula.

- Bake in the preheated oven for 75-90 minutes, or until a toothpick inserted into the center comes out clean.

5. **Soak the Fruitcake:**
    - While the fruitcake is still warm, poke holes in the top with a toothpick or skewer.
    - Pour 1/4 cup of brandy, rum, or orange juice evenly over the top of the warm cake. Let it cool completely in the pan.

6. **Store the Fruitcake:**
    - Once cooled, remove the fruitcake from the pan and wrap it tightly in plastic wrap or aluminum foil.
    - Store the wrapped fruitcake in a cool, dark place for at least a few days before serving to allow the flavors to meld and develop. You can continue to brush the cake with additional brandy, rum, or orange juice every few days to enhance the flavors.

7. **Serve:**
    - Fruitcake can be enjoyed on its own or with a cup of tea or coffee. It also makes a wonderful gift during the holiday season.

This homemade fruitcake recipe yields a moist and flavorful cake filled with the richness of dried fruits and nuts. It's a classic dessert that brings warmth and nostalgia to any occasion!

Chocolate Souffle

Ingredients:

- 4 ounces (115g) bittersweet chocolate, chopped
- 1/4 cup (60ml) heavy cream
- 3 large egg yolks
- 1/4 cup (50g) granulated sugar, plus extra for coating ramekins
- Pinch of salt
- 4 large egg whites
- 1/4 teaspoon cream of tartar (optional, for stabilizing egg whites)
- Butter, for greasing ramekins

For Serving:

- Powdered sugar, for dusting
- Whipped cream or vanilla ice cream (optional)

Instructions:

1. **Prepare the Ramekins:**
   - Preheat your oven to 375°F (190°C). Butter the bottoms and sides of 4-6 (depending on size) 6-ounce ramekins or soufflé dishes. Sprinkle granulated sugar into each ramekin, rotating to coat the buttered surfaces evenly. Tap out any excess sugar.
2. **Melt the Chocolate:**
   - In a heatproof bowl set over a pan of simmering water (double boiler), melt the chopped bittersweet chocolate with the heavy cream, stirring occasionally until smooth. Remove from heat and set aside to cool slightly.
3. **Prepare the Base:**
   - In a large mixing bowl, whisk together the egg yolks, granulated sugar, and a pinch of salt until pale and slightly thickened.
   - Gradually whisk the melted chocolate mixture into the egg yolk mixture until well combined. Set aside.
4. **Whip the Egg Whites:**
   - In a clean, dry mixing bowl (preferably metal or glass), beat the egg whites with a hand mixer or stand mixer on medium speed until foamy.
   - Add the cream of tartar (if using) and continue beating on medium-high speed until soft peaks form. Gradually add the remaining granulated sugar, about 1 tablespoon at a time, while continuing to beat, until stiff peaks form.
5. **Fold and Bake:**
   - Gently fold one-third of the beaten egg whites into the chocolate mixture to lighten it. Then, carefully fold in the remaining egg whites until no streaks remain, being careful not to deflate the mixture.

- Spoon the soufflé mixture into the prepared ramekins, filling them almost to the top. Smooth the tops with a spatula.
6. **Bake the Soufflés:**
    - Place the filled ramekins on a baking sheet and transfer to the preheated oven. Bake for 12-15 minutes (depending on your oven and the size of the soufflés), until puffed and set on top. The centers should still be slightly jiggly.
7. **Serve Immediately:**
    - Dust the tops of the soufflés with powdered sugar and serve immediately, while they are still puffed and airy.
    - Optionally, serve with whipped cream or vanilla ice cream on the side for a delightful contrast of flavors and textures.

Chocolate soufflé is best enjoyed right out of the oven when it's at its tallest and most impressive. It's a perfect dessert for special occasions or any time you want to impress with a classic French delicacy!

Cherry Pie

Ingredients:

For the Pie Crust:

- 2 and 1/2 cups (315g) all-purpose flour
- 1 tablespoon granulated sugar
- 1 teaspoon salt
- 1 cup (225g) unsalted butter, cold and cut into cubes
- 6-8 tablespoons ice water

For the Cherry Filling:

- 4 cups (about 600g) fresh or frozen cherries, pitted
- 3/4 cup (150g) granulated sugar
- 1/4 cup (30g) cornstarch
- 1 tablespoon fresh lemon juice
- 1/4 teaspoon almond extract (optional)
- 1/4 teaspoon vanilla extract
- Pinch of salt
- 1 tablespoon unsalted butter, cut into small pieces

For Assembly:

- 1 egg, beaten (for egg wash)
- Coarse sugar, for sprinkling (optional)

Instructions:

1. **Make the Pie Crust:**
   - In a large bowl, whisk together the flour, sugar, and salt. Add the cold, cubed butter.
   - Using a pastry cutter or your fingertips, work the butter into the flour mixture until it resembles coarse crumbs with some larger pieces of butter remaining.
   - Gradually add ice water, 1 tablespoon at a time, mixing with a fork or your hands, until the dough just begins to come together. It should hold together when squeezed but not be sticky.
   - Divide the dough into two equal portions, shape each into a disk, and wrap tightly in plastic wrap. Refrigerate for at least 1 hour, or overnight.
2. **Prepare the Cherry Filling:**
   - In a large bowl, combine the pitted cherries, granulated sugar, cornstarch, lemon juice, almond extract (if using), vanilla extract, and a pinch of salt. Toss gently to combine and let it sit for about 15 minutes to macerate.
3. **Preheat your oven to 400°F (200°C).**
4. **Roll Out the Pie Crust:**

- On a lightly floured surface, roll out one disk of chilled pie dough into a circle about 12 inches in diameter. Carefully transfer it to a 9-inch pie dish. Trim any excess dough, leaving about a 1-inch overhang.
5. **Fill the Pie:**
    - Spoon the cherry filling into the prepared pie crust, spreading it evenly. Dot the filling with pieces of butter.
6. **Top the Pie:**
    - Roll out the second disk of chilled pie dough into a circle about 12 inches in diameter. Carefully place it over the filled pie. Trim any excess dough, leaving a 1-inch overhang.
    - Fold the overhanging dough under itself, creating a thick edge that rests on the rim of the pie dish. Crimp the edges with your fingers or use a fork to seal.
7. **Bake the Pie:**
    - Brush the top of the pie with beaten egg and sprinkle with coarse sugar, if desired.
    - Cut a few slits in the top crust to allow steam to escape during baking.
    - Place the pie on a baking sheet (to catch any drips) and bake in the preheated oven for 45-55 minutes, or until the crust is golden brown and the filling is bubbly.
8. **Cool and Serve:**
    - Allow the cherry pie to cool on a wire rack for at least 2 hours before serving. This helps the filling set.
    - Serve slices of cherry pie at room temperature or slightly warmed, optionally with a scoop of vanilla ice cream or a dollop of whipped cream.

Enjoy this homemade cherry pie with its juicy, flavorful filling and buttery crust—a perfect dessert for any occasion, especially during cherry season!

Irish Soda Bread

Ingredients:

- 4 cups (500g) all-purpose flour
- 1 tablespoon granulated sugar
- 1 teaspoon baking soda
- 1 teaspoon salt
- 4 tablespoons (55g) unsalted butter, cold and cut into small pieces
- 1 and 1/2 cups (360ml) buttermilk (or substitute with 1 and 1/2 cups milk mixed with 1 and 1/2 tablespoons vinegar or lemon juice, let sit for 5 minutes to sour)

Optional add-ins:

- 1 cup (150g) raisins or currants
- 1 tablespoon caraway seeds

Instructions:

1. Preheat your oven to 425°F (220°C). Line a baking sheet with parchment paper or lightly grease it.
2. In a large bowl, whisk together the flour, sugar, baking soda, and salt.
3. Add the cold butter pieces to the flour mixture. Using your fingertips or a pastry cutter, work the butter into the flour until the mixture resembles coarse crumbs. If using, stir in the raisins or currants and caraway seeds at this point.
4. Make a well in the center of the flour mixture. Pour the buttermilk into the well.
5. Using a wooden spoon or your hands, stir the mixture until it just comes together into a sticky dough. Be careful not to overmix.
6. Turn the dough out onto a lightly floured surface. Gently knead the dough a few times, just until it forms a cohesive ball.
7. Shape the dough into a round loaf. Place it on the prepared baking sheet.
8. Using a sharp knife, score a cross (X) on the top of the loaf. This helps the bread expand evenly as it bakes and is a traditional Irish soda bread mark.
9. Bake in the preheated oven for 35-40 minutes, or until the bread is golden brown and sounds hollow when tapped on the bottom.
10. Transfer the bread to a wire rack to cool completely before slicing.
11. Serve the Irish Soda Bread with butter, jam, or alongside soups and stews. It's best enjoyed fresh on the day it's baked but can be stored in an airtight container for a day or two.

Irish Soda Bread is a rustic, versatile bread that pairs well with both sweet and savory toppings. Its simplicity makes it a favorite for quick baking sessions and as an accompaniment to meals throughout the day. Enjoy the warm, comforting flavors of homemade Irish Soda Bread!

Mille-Feuille (Napoleon)

Ingredients:

For the Puff Pastry:

- 1 sheet of store-bought puff pastry (about 12x15 inches), thawed if frozen

For the Pastry Cream:

- 2 cups (480ml) whole milk
- 1/2 cup (100g) granulated sugar
- 4 large egg yolks
- 1/4 cup (30g) cornstarch
- 1/2 teaspoon vanilla extract
- Pinch of salt
- 2 tablespoons (30g) unsalted butter, cut into small pieces

For Assembly:

- Powdered sugar, for dusting
- Optional: Dark chocolate for decoration, fresh berries, or whipped cream

Instructions:

1. **Prepare the Puff Pastry:**
   - Preheat your oven to 400°F (200°C). Line a baking sheet with parchment paper.
   - Roll out the puff pastry on a lightly floured surface to about 1/8 inch thickness. Trim the edges to make neat rectangles (if necessary) and prick the surface all over with a fork.
   - Place the pastry on the prepared baking sheet and bake for 15-20 minutes, or until golden brown and puffed. Remove from the oven and let it cool completely on a wire rack.

2. **Make the Pastry Cream:**
   - In a medium saucepan, heat the milk over medium heat until steaming (do not boil). Remove from heat.
   - In a separate bowl, whisk together the sugar, egg yolks, cornstarch, vanilla extract, and salt until smooth and creamy.
   - Gradually whisk the hot milk into the egg mixture, a little at a time, to temper the eggs.
   - Return the mixture to the saucepan and cook over medium heat, whisking constantly, until thickened and bubbly, about 2-3 minutes.
   - Remove from heat and whisk in the butter until melted and smooth.
   - Transfer the pastry cream to a bowl and cover with plastic wrap directly on the surface to prevent a skin from forming. Refrigerate until chilled and thickened, about 1-2 hours.

3. **Assemble the Mille-Feuille:**
    - Once the puff pastry has cooled completely, carefully cut it into equal-sized rectangles.
    - Place one rectangle of puff pastry on a serving plate. Spread a layer of pastry cream evenly over the pastry.
    - Top with another rectangle of puff pastry and press down gently.
    - Repeat the layering process with the remaining puff pastry and pastry cream, ending with a layer of puff pastry on top.
4. **Decorate:**
    - Dust the top layer of puff pastry with powdered sugar.
    - If desired, melt dark chocolate and drizzle it over the top layer of the mille-feuille for decoration.
    - Optional: Garnish with fresh berries or serve with whipped cream on the side.
5. **Chill and Serve:**
    - Refrigerate the assembled mille-feuille for at least 1 hour before serving to allow the layers to set.
    - Slice carefully with a sharp knife and serve chilled. Enjoy the delicate layers of flaky puff pastry and creamy pastry cream in this elegant French dessert!

Mille-feuille (Napoleon) is a delightful pastry that impresses with its layers and flavors. It's perfect for special occasions or whenever you want to treat yourself to a taste of French patisserie at home.

Palmiers

Ingredients:

- 1 sheet of store-bought puff pastry (about 12x15 inches), thawed if frozen
- 1 cup (200g) granulated sugar
- Pinch of salt

Instructions:

1. **Preheat your oven to 400°F (200°C). Line a baking sheet with parchment paper.**
2. **Prepare the Palmiers:**
   - Sprinkle half of the sugar onto a clean work surface. Unroll the puff pastry sheet onto the sugar.
   - Sprinkle the remaining sugar evenly over the top of the puff pastry sheet. Use a rolling pin to gently press the sugar into the pastry.
   - Fold the two opposite sides of the puff pastry sheet towards the center, stopping halfway so they meet. Repeat so the folds meet in the center again.
   - Fold one half over the other half like closing a book. This will create multiple layers of sugar and pastry.
3. **Slice and Bake:**
   - Using a sharp knife, slice the rolled pastry crosswise into 1/2-inch thick slices.
   - Place the slices on the prepared baking sheet, cut-side down, spacing them about 1 inch apart.
4. **Bake:**
   - Bake in the preheated oven for 12-15 minutes, or until the palmiers are golden brown and caramelized.
5. **Cool and Serve:**
   - Remove the palmiers from the oven and let them cool on the baking sheet for a few minutes.
   - Transfer the palmiers to a wire rack to cool completely before serving.

Palmiers are best enjoyed fresh but can be stored in an airtight container at room temperature for a few days. They make a delightful treat with coffee or tea, and their elegant appearance makes them perfect for serving at parties or as a homemade gift. Enjoy the crispy, caramelized goodness of these homemade palmiers!

Lemon Pound Cake

Ingredients:

- 1 cup (226g) unsalted butter, softened
- 1 and 1/2 cups (300g) granulated sugar
- 4 large eggs, room temperature
- 2 teaspoons vanilla extract
- 2 tablespoons lemon zest (from about 2-3 lemons)
- 3 tablespoons fresh lemon juice
- 2 cups (250g) all-purpose flour
- 1 teaspoon baking powder
- 1/2 teaspoon baking soda
- 1/2 teaspoon salt
- 1/2 cup (120ml) sour cream or plain yogurt

For the Lemon Glaze:

- 1 cup (120g) powdered sugar
- 2-3 tablespoons fresh lemon juice

Instructions:

1. Preheat your oven to 350°F (175°C). Grease and flour a 9x5-inch loaf pan or line it with parchment paper.
2. In a large mixing bowl, cream together the softened butter and granulated sugar until light and fluffy, about 3-4 minutes.
3. Add the eggs one at a time, beating well after each addition.
4. Mix in the vanilla extract, lemon zest, and fresh lemon juice until well combined.
5. In a separate bowl, whisk together the flour, baking powder, baking soda, and salt.
6. Gradually add the dry ingredients to the wet ingredients, alternating with the sour cream or yogurt, beginning and ending with the flour mixture. Mix until just combined.
7. Pour the batter into the prepared loaf pan and smooth the top with a spatula.
8. Bake in the preheated oven for 55-65 minutes, or until a toothpick inserted into the center of the cake comes out clean or with a few moist crumbs.
9. While the cake is baking, prepare the lemon glaze: In a small bowl, whisk together the powdered sugar and fresh lemon juice until smooth. Adjust the consistency by adding more sugar or juice as needed.
10. Remove the cake from the oven and let it cool in the pan for 10-15 minutes. Then, remove from the pan and transfer to a wire rack set over a baking sheet or parchment paper.
11. While the cake is still warm, drizzle the lemon glaze over the top of the cake. Allow the glaze to set before slicing and serving.
12. Slice and Serve: Enjoy slices of lemon pound cake with a cup of tea or coffee. The tangy lemon flavor and moist texture make it a delightful treat for any occasion.

This lemon pound cake can be stored in an airtight container at room temperature for up to 3 days, or in the refrigerator for up to 1 week. It also freezes well—wrap tightly in plastic wrap and foil before freezing for up to 3 months. Enjoy the bright flavors of lemon in this classic pound cake!

Popovers

Ingredients:

- 2 cups (240g) all-purpose flour
- 1 teaspoon salt
- 3 large eggs, at room temperature
- 2 cups (480ml) whole milk, at room temperature
- 2 tablespoons unsalted butter, melted
- Butter or non-stick cooking spray, for greasing the popover pan or muffin tin

Instructions:

1. Preheat your oven to 450°F (230°C). Place a popover pan or a standard 12-cup muffin tin in the oven to preheat as well.
2. In a large bowl, whisk together the flour and salt.
3. In another bowl or large measuring cup, whisk together the eggs, milk, and melted butter until well combined.
4. Gradually add the wet ingredients to the dry ingredients, whisking until smooth and no lumps remain. The batter should be thin and pourable, similar to heavy cream consistency.
5. Carefully remove the hot popover pan or muffin tin from the oven. Grease the cups with butter or non-stick cooking spray.
6. Pour the batter into the cups, filling each cup about halfway.
7. Bake at 450°F (230°C) for 15 minutes. Then, without opening the oven door, reduce the oven temperature to 350°F (175°C) and bake for an additional 20-25 minutes, until the popovers are golden brown and puffed up.
8. Remove the popovers from the oven and immediately pierce each popover with a sharp knife or skewer to release steam and help them keep their shape.
9. Serve immediately while warm. Popovers are delicious with butter and jam, or as a savory treat with cheese or herbs.
10. Optional Variations:
- For a savory twist, add grated cheese, herbs (such as thyme or rosemary), or black pepper to the batter before baking.
- For sweet popovers, you can sprinkle cinnamon sugar on top after baking or serve with a drizzle of honey.

Popovers are best enjoyed fresh out of the oven when they are light and airy. They are perfect for breakfast, brunch, or as a side dish with soups and salads. Enjoy the simple elegance of homemade popovers!

Cannoli

Ingredients:

For the Cannoli Shells:

- 2 cups (250g) all-purpose flour
- 2 tablespoons granulated sugar
- 1/4 teaspoon salt
- 2 tablespoons unsalted butter, softened
- 1/2 cup (120ml) sweet Marsala wine (or white wine)
- 1 egg white, lightly beaten
- Vegetable oil, for frying

For the Cannoli Filling:

- 2 cups (475g) whole milk ricotta cheese, drained if necessary
- 1/2 cup (60g) powdered sugar
- 1/2 teaspoon vanilla extract
- 1/4 cup (30g) mini chocolate chips, optional
- Powdered sugar, for dusting

Instructions:

Making the Cannoli Shells:

1. In a large bowl, whisk together the flour, sugar, and salt.
2. Add the softened butter and mix until crumbly.
3. Gradually add the Marsala wine, stirring until the dough comes together.
4. Knead the dough on a lightly floured surface until smooth and elastic, about 5-7 minutes.
5. Cover the dough with a damp cloth or plastic wrap and let it rest for at least 30 minutes.
6. Roll out the dough on a lightly floured surface until very thin, about 1/8 inch thick.
7. Using a 4-inch round cutter or glass, cut out circles from the dough.
8. Wrap each circle of dough around a metal cannoli tube, overlapping slightly, and seal the edges with the beaten egg white.
9. Heat about 2 inches of vegetable oil in a heavy-bottomed pot to 350°F (175°C).
10. Carefully fry the cannoli shells in batches until golden brown and crispy, about 2-3 minutes.
11. Remove the shells using tongs and place them on paper towels to drain and cool.
12. Once cool enough to handle, carefully slide the shells off the tubes and set them aside to cool completely.

Making the Cannoli Filling:

1. In a medium bowl, combine the ricotta cheese, powdered sugar, and vanilla extract.
2. Stir until smooth and creamy.

3. Fold in the mini chocolate chips, if using.

Assembling the Cannoli:

1. Using a pastry bag fitted with a large star tip (or a spoon), fill each cannoli shell with the ricotta filling from both ends.
2. Dust the filled cannoli with powdered sugar.
3. Optional: Garnish with additional mini chocolate chips or chopped pistachios.
4. Serve immediately or refrigerate until ready to serve.

Enjoy these homemade cannoli as a delightful dessert or treat for special occasions. The combination of crispy shells and creamy filling makes them a favorite Italian pastry that's sure to impress!

Black Forest Cake

Ingredients:

For the Chocolate Cake Layers:

- 1 and 3/4 cups (220g) all-purpose flour
- 3/4 cup (75g) unsweetened cocoa powder
- 1 and 1/2 teaspoons baking powder
- 1 and 1/2 teaspoons baking soda
- 1/2 teaspoon salt
- 2 cups (400g) granulated sugar
- 2 large eggs, at room temperature
- 1 cup (240ml) whole milk
- 1/2 cup (120ml) vegetable oil
- 2 teaspoons vanilla extract
- 1 cup (240ml) boiling water

For the Cherry Filling:

- 1 (15-ounce) can pitted cherries in syrup, drained (reserve syrup)
- 1 tablespoon cornstarch
- 2 tablespoons granulated sugar
- 1 tablespoon cherry brandy (Kirsch), optional

For the Whipped Cream Frosting:

- 3 cups (720ml) heavy cream, chilled
- 1/2 cup (60g) powdered sugar
- 1 teaspoon vanilla extract

For Assembly:

- Chocolate shavings or curls, for decoration
- Additional cherries, for garnish (optional)

Instructions:

1. Prepare the Chocolate Cake Layers:

- Preheat your oven to 350°F (175°C). Grease and flour three 9-inch round cake pans, or line them with parchment paper.
- In a large bowl, sift together the flour, cocoa powder, baking powder, baking soda, and salt.
- In another bowl, whisk together the sugar, eggs, milk, vegetable oil, and vanilla extract until well combined.

- Gradually add the wet ingredients to the dry ingredients, mixing until smooth.
- Stir in the boiling water, mixing until the batter is well combined and smooth. The batter will be thin.
- Divide the batter evenly among the prepared cake pans.
- Bake for 25-30 minutes, or until a toothpick inserted into the center of the cakes comes out clean.
- Remove from the oven and let the cakes cool in the pans for 10 minutes before transferring them to wire racks to cool completely.

2. Make the Cherry Filling:

- In a small saucepan, combine the drained cherries, reserved cherry syrup, cornstarch, and sugar.
- Cook over medium heat, stirring constantly, until the mixture thickens and comes to a boil.
- Remove from heat and stir in the cherry brandy, if using.
- Let the cherry filling cool completely before using it in the cake.

3. Prepare the Whipped Cream Frosting:

- In a chilled mixing bowl, beat the heavy cream, powdered sugar, and vanilla extract until stiff peaks form.

4. Assemble the Black Forest Cake:

- Place one cake layer on a serving plate. Spread a layer of whipped cream frosting over the cake layer.
- Spoon a generous amount of cherry filling over the whipped cream.
- Place another cake layer on top and repeat the layers: whipped cream frosting, cherry filling.
- Top with the third cake layer and frost the top and sides of the cake with the remaining whipped cream frosting.

5. Decorate the Cake:

- Garnish the top of the cake with chocolate shavings or curls.
- Optionally, garnish with additional cherries on top.

6. Chill the Cake:

- Refrigerate the cake for at least 1-2 hours before serving to allow the flavors to meld together.

7. Serve and Enjoy:

- Slice and serve the Black Forest Cake chilled. It's a decadent dessert that's sure to impress with its layers of chocolate, cherries, and creamy whipped topping.

This homemade Black Forest Cake is perfect for celebrations or special occasions, showcasing the classic flavors and textures that make it a beloved dessert worldwide.

Buttermilk Biscuits

Ingredients:

- 2 cups (250g) all-purpose flour, plus extra for dusting
- 1 tablespoon baking powder
- 1/2 teaspoon baking soda
- 1 teaspoon salt
- 6 tablespoons (85g) unsalted butter, cold and cut into small cubes
- 1 cup (240ml) buttermilk, cold

Instructions:

1. Preheat your oven to 450°F (230°C). Line a baking sheet with parchment paper.
2. In a large bowl, whisk together the flour, baking powder, baking soda, and salt.
3. Add the cold butter cubes to the flour mixture. Using a pastry cutter, fork, or your fingertips, cut the butter into the flour until the mixture resembles coarse crumbs with some pea-sized pieces of butter remaining.
4. Make a well in the center of the flour mixture. Pour the cold buttermilk into the well.
5. Using a spatula or wooden spoon, gently stir the mixture until the dough just begins to come together. Be careful not to overmix; the dough should be shaggy and moist.
6. Turn the dough out onto a lightly floured surface. Pat the dough into a rectangle or square, about 1-inch thick.
7. Fold the dough in half and pat it out again to 1-inch thickness. Repeat this folding process 2-3 more times. This helps create layers in the biscuits.
8. Using a floured 2-inch round biscuit cutter, cut out biscuits from the dough. Press straight down without twisting the cutter to ensure even rising.
9. Place the biscuits on the prepared baking sheet, spacing them about 1 inch apart for crisp edges or touching for softer edges.
10. Gather any remaining dough scraps, gently press them together, and cut out more biscuits until all the dough is used.
11. Bake in the preheated oven for 10-12 minutes, or until the biscuits are golden brown on top.
12. Remove from the oven and brush the tops of the biscuits with melted butter, if desired.
13. Serve warm, split open and spread with butter, honey, jam, or gravy.

Enjoy these homemade buttermilk biscuits for breakfast, brunch, or as a comforting side to soups and stews. They are best served fresh from the oven while still warm and fluffy!

Danish Pastry

Ingredients:

For the Dough:

- 2 and 1/4 cups (280g) all-purpose flour
- 1/4 cup (50g) granulated sugar
- 1 teaspoon salt
- 1 packet (2 and 1/4 teaspoons) active dry yeast
- 1/2 cup (120ml) warm milk (about 110°F or 45°C)
- 1/4 cup (60ml) warm water
- 1 large egg, room temperature
- 1/2 cup (115g) unsalted butter, cold, cut into small cubes

For the Butter Block:

- 1 cup (230g) unsalted butter, cold

Instructions:

1. Make the Dough:

- In a large mixing bowl, whisk together the flour, sugar, salt, and yeast.
- In a separate bowl or measuring cup, whisk together the warm milk, warm water, and egg.
- Pour the wet ingredients into the dry ingredients and mix until a rough dough forms.
- Turn the dough out onto a lightly floured surface and knead for about 5-7 minutes, until smooth and elastic.
- Shape the dough into a square, wrap it in plastic wrap, and refrigerate for 30 minutes.

2. Prepare the Butter Block:

- While the dough is chilling, prepare the butter block. Place the cold butter between two sheets of parchment paper or plastic wrap.
- Use a rolling pin to pound and flatten the butter into a square, about 1/2 inch thick.
- Refrigerate the butter block until firm, but still pliable.

3. Laminate the Dough:

- On a lightly floured surface, roll out the chilled dough into a square, about 10 inches (25cm) across.
- Place the chilled butter block in the center of the dough square at a diagonal.
- Fold the corners of the dough over the butter block, stretching and sealing the edges to fully encase the butter.

- Roll out the dough into a rectangle, about 12x20 inches (30x50cm). Fold the dough into thirds like a business letter.
- Turn the dough 90 degrees, roll it out again into a rectangle, and fold it into thirds. This completes one "turn."
- Wrap the dough in plastic wrap and refrigerate for at least 30 minutes.
- Repeat the rolling, folding, and chilling process two more times for a total of three turns.

4. Shape and Bake the Danish Pastry:

- After the final turn, wrap the dough and refrigerate overnight or for at least 4 hours before using.
- When ready to bake, roll out the chilled dough to about 1/4 inch thick.
- Cut the dough into desired shapes (rectangles, squares, circles) for your chosen Danish pastries.
- Place the shaped pastries on a baking sheet lined with parchment paper, leaving space between them for rising.
- Cover the pastries loosely with plastic wrap and let them rise at room temperature for 30-60 minutes, until puffy.
- Preheat your oven to 400°F (200°C).
- Brush the pastries with an egg wash (1 egg beaten with 1 tablespoon of water).
- Bake the pastries for 15-20 minutes, until golden brown and flaky.
- Remove from the oven and let cool slightly on a wire rack.

5. Optional: Fill and Glaze the Pastries:

- Once cooled, you can fill the pastries with pastry cream, fruit preserves, almond filling, or cheese filling.
- Drizzle with glaze or sprinkle with powdered sugar, if desired.

Enjoy your homemade Danish pastries! They are best served fresh, with a cup of coffee or tea, and make a delightful treat for breakfast or brunch.

Sticky Buns

Ingredients:

For the Dough:

- 4 cups (500g) all-purpose flour
- 1/4 cup (50g) granulated sugar
- 1 teaspoon salt
- 2 and 1/4 teaspoons active dry yeast (1 packet)
- 1 cup (240ml) warm milk (about 110°F or 45°C)
- 1/4 cup (60ml) warm water
- 1/3 cup (75g) unsalted butter, softened
- 2 large eggs, room temperature

For the Filling:

- 1/2 cup (100g) packed light brown sugar
- 2 teaspoons ground cinnamon
- 1/4 cup (60g) unsalted butter, melted
- 1 cup (120g) chopped pecans or walnuts (optional)

For the Sticky Topping:

- 1 cup (200g) packed light brown sugar
- 1/2 cup (115g) unsalted butter
- 1/4 cup (60ml) light corn syrup
- 1 cup (120g) chopped pecans or walnuts (optional)

Instructions:

1. Make the Dough:

- In a large mixing bowl or the bowl of a stand mixer fitted with the dough hook, combine 3 cups of flour, sugar, salt, and yeast.
- In a separate bowl or measuring cup, whisk together the warm milk, warm water, softened butter, and eggs.
- Pour the wet ingredients into the dry ingredients and mix until a soft dough forms.
- Gradually add the remaining 1 cup of flour, a little at a time, until the dough comes together and pulls away from the sides of the bowl.
- Knead the dough on a lightly floured surface or with the dough hook on medium speed for 5-7 minutes, until smooth and elastic.
- Place the dough in a greased bowl, turning once to grease the top. Cover with plastic wrap or a clean kitchen towel and let it rise in a warm place until doubled in size, about 1-2 hours.

2. Prepare the Sticky Topping:

- In a medium saucepan, combine the brown sugar, butter, and corn syrup.
- Cook over medium heat, stirring constantly, until the mixture is smooth and the sugar has dissolved, about 3-5 minutes.
- Pour the sticky topping into the bottom of a greased 9x13-inch baking dish, spreading it evenly.
- Sprinkle the chopped nuts evenly over the sticky topping, if using.

3. Assemble the Sticky Buns:

- Punch down the risen dough and roll it out on a lightly floured surface into a rectangle, about 18x12 inches.
- In a small bowl, mix together the brown sugar and cinnamon for the filling.
- Brush the melted butter over the rolled-out dough, leaving a small border around the edges.
- Sprinkle the cinnamon-sugar mixture evenly over the buttered dough.
- Sprinkle the chopped nuts evenly over the cinnamon-sugar mixture, if using.
- Starting from the long edge, tightly roll up the dough into a log. Pinch the seam to seal.
- Cut the dough into 12 equal pieces using a sharp knife or dental floss. Place the cut rolls in the prepared baking dish, cut side down, spacing them evenly over the sticky topping.
- Cover the baking dish loosely with plastic wrap or a clean kitchen towel and let the rolls rise in a warm place until puffy and doubled in size, about 30-60 minutes.

4. Bake the Sticky Buns:

- Preheat your oven to 375°F (190°C).
- Once the rolls have risen, bake them in the preheated oven for 25-30 minutes, or until golden brown and cooked through.
- Remove from the oven and let the sticky buns cool in the pan for 5 minutes.
- Invert the sticky buns onto a serving platter or a parchment-lined tray immediately (be careful of the hot caramel topping).
- Allow the sticky buns to cool slightly before serving. The caramel topping will be hot and sticky, so handle with care.

5. Serve and Enjoy:

- Serve the sticky buns warm. Enjoy the sweet, gooey caramel topping and cinnamon-nut filling!

These homemade sticky buns are perfect for breakfast or brunch, and they're sure to impress with their decadent flavors and comforting aroma.

Pita Bread

Ingredients:

- 3 cups (375g) all-purpose flour
- 1 teaspoon salt
- 1 tablespoon granulated sugar
- 2 teaspoons instant yeast
- 1 cup (240ml) warm water (about 110°F or 45°C)
- 2 tablespoons olive oil

Instructions:

1. **Mixing the Dough:**
    - In a large bowl, combine the flour, salt, sugar, and instant yeast.
    - Make a well in the center of the dry ingredients and pour in the warm water and olive oil.
    - Stir the mixture with a wooden spoon or mix with your hands until a shaggy dough forms.
    - Turn the dough out onto a lightly floured surface and knead for about 8-10 minutes, or until the dough is smooth, elastic, and slightly tacky.
2. **First Rise:**
    - Place the kneaded dough in a lightly oiled bowl, turning once to coat the dough with oil.
    - Cover the bowl with a clean kitchen towel or plastic wrap.
    - Let the dough rise in a warm place for about 1-1.5 hours, or until doubled in size.
3. **Shaping the Pita Bread:**
    - Once the dough has doubled in size, punch it down to release the air.
    - Divide the dough into 8 equal pieces and shape each piece into a smooth ball.
    - Cover the dough balls with a kitchen towel and let them rest for 10-15 minutes.
4. **Baking the Pita Bread:**
    - Preheat your oven to 475°F (245°C) with a baking stone or overturned baking sheet inside to heat up.
    - On a lightly floured surface, roll out each dough ball into a circle or oval shape, about 1/4 inch thick.
    - Carefully transfer the rolled-out dough to the preheated baking stone or baking sheet. You can bake 2-3 pitas at a time, depending on the size of your baking surface.
    - Bake the pitas for 3-4 minutes, or until they puff up and the bottoms are lightly golden.
    - Flip the pitas using tongs or a spatula and bake for an additional 2 minutes, until the other side is lightly golden and the bread is cooked through.
5. **Cooling and Serving:**
    - Remove the baked pitas from the oven and transfer them to a wire rack to cool slightly.

- Cover the pitas with a clean kitchen towel to keep them soft and warm.
- Serve the pita bread warm or at room temperature. They're perfect for stuffing with falafel, grilled meats, fresh vegetables, or dipping into hummus and other dips.

Enjoy your homemade pita bread fresh and warm. Store any leftovers in an airtight container or zip-top bag at room temperature for up to 2 days, or freeze for longer storage. Just reheat in a toaster or oven before serving to revive their freshness.

www.ingramcontent.com/pod-product-compliance
Lightning Source LLC
LaVergne TN
LVHW081608060526
838201LV00054B/2137